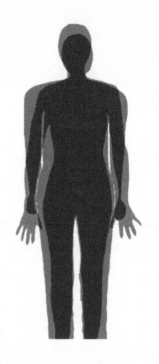

RESTRICTED

a novel of half-truths

JENNIFER KINSEL

An independently published work.

First edition.

   ISBN: 145152160X
EAN-13: 9781451521603

Printed in the United States of America.

*For those who know how it feels to be restricted,
and for those who have broken free.*

ACKNOWLEDGMENTS

There are many people who I would like to thank individually, and it would be impossible to name everyone in this small space. But if we have crossed paths, you have surely played a role in my journey.

My therapist, Kristin Grasso, Psy.D., for providing a listening ear, for believing in me, and for challenging me in the best ways possible. For the safety and empathy that's given during each session, I'm very grateful.

The rest of my treatment team, past and present, especially Amanda Bechtel, MS, ATR, LCPC; Hannah Huguenin, MS, RD, LDN; and Mindy Lais, Psy.D.; for giving me the tools to help dig myself out of the eating disorder, and for pushing me when I wanted to go no further – even though I didn't always agree at the time.

Those who I've met in treatment, for giving me inspiration and insight. Each of you are amazing and I'm certain we will all make it to the other side. I've learned from every one of you; I hope I've taught you something, as well.

My mom and dad, Beverly and George, for standing by me through the years. Although I know it's hard to completely understand things from my side, the effort has been made to learn with me. I know that I'll always have support.

PREFACE

I often wonder how others react to serious topics such as eating disorders. In today's society, eating disorders have somehow become glamorized in the media. It has become the "it" thing to have among celebrities. Those who do admit to having a problem sometimes seek treatment, and the rest of the world only hears that she (or he) is now cured after a stint in a top-notch treatment center.

Only, it rarely works that way. Those suffering are lucky if they can enter treatment and even luckier if their eating disorder does not still rule their life after treatment. Insurance companies are hesitant to cover those asking for help, and in many cases, patients are kicked out of the facility before they are ready to leave. Out of all psychiatric illnesses, eating disorders have the highest mortality rate, and many suffer throughout their entire life. Not all who battle an eating disorder are on their death bed like those shown on television for shock value. I am quite baffled at the variety of people I have met through treatment; those who could easily be your daughter, your next door neighbor, your idol. Eating disorders do not discriminate between sex, race, social status, religion, or sexual orientation.

I have written this book based upon my own experience in battling an eating disorder. While I am not recovered, I am in recovery. I know very well the evil, yet tantalizing path an eating disorder can lead. Although this is not a memoir, most of the contents hold some truth. This book is not a glamorized portrait of eating disorders; it is a real glimpse into the pain and suffering behind so many smiles trying to hide it all. It's a look at the difficult and trying process of recovery.

PROLOGUE

I thought that once I had lost the weight, I would feel better about myself and maybe I would be something special. Well, I have lost weight, I do not feel better about myself, and I am still nothing special.

I glanced up from my notebook to see a fidgeting girl across the room, tapping her foot on the floor and shaking her leg to an imaginary, silent beat. Her anxiety disturbed others and it was distracting me from the assignment that was passed around for the group to quietly work on. Like yawning, it seemed that when one person fidgeted, everyone else caught on, and soon numerous legs were all simultaneously bouncing on the ground. Tap. Tap. Tap. How was I supposed to concentrate on my work with jumping legs in my view? My thoughts were not focused on the worksheet that was before me. I was trapped inside a very big, dark room with eight other girls and women, ranging in age from 15 to 43. We were all there for the same reason, yet we all arrived at that point by taking different paths. My mind drifted to a scenario, sparked by the worksheet's questions.

She swung her tiny arms around and felt the cool breeze against her skin. Her legs held her little body upright as she turned and gently pointed her toes to the ground. The smile on her face showed how proud she was for showing off the simple dance move she learned in ballet class the previous week. A three year old was sometimes hard to teach, yet she was able to pick up a lesson very quickly. Her mother clapped as her daughter finished and went back inside to finish cooking dinner, while the young girl stayed outside to keep practicing.

The leotard the girl was wearing reflected back at her like a mirror on the glass door. She was fascinated at the image and stared into the window pane, analyzing the outfit and her body. A full length image gave her a very different view of herself, a view she was not used to seeing. Her arms appeared shorter, her legs appeared thicker, her hair appeared darker. Questioning the validity of the reflection, she tried to judge herself by seeing her body from her eyes. Looking down, she noticed that her stomach was not as flat as she thought it should be. She consciously sucked in, using her stomach muscles to make her appear thinner.

"I'm fat.," she thought. Before that moment, the thought never crossed her mind. A bit of confusion entered her mind, not from questioning the critique itself, but from the lack of self-criticism before that moment.

Self criticism was not uncommon for her to hear, as she heard it quite often within her household and family circle. Often, her mother would find herself looking into a mirror and saying, "Ugh, I need to lose some weight." The little girl did not recognize that her mother needed to lose weight, but she recognized that the comment made was self loathing, in a way that something needed to be changed in order for her to feel better.

Was she even aware of what "fat" was? At three

years old, most children were worrying about which lollipop to choose or which doll Santa Claus would bring for Christmas that year. But she was different and she worried about many things that other three year old's never thought about. Feeling fat was not even necessarily a logical response to seeing herself in the mirror. Feeling fat was quickly being learned as a way to describe being uncomfortable, being overwhelmed, being anxious. She did not know that feeling fat had nothing to do with her physical self at all, but it would play a huge role in the years ahead.

The only thing more sad than imagining an innocent three year old thinking herself as fat, was admitting that I was that three year old. One of my earliest memories was dancing around in a leotard and sucking in my stomach because I was not happy with my body. It saddened me because I knew that was not how three year old's were supposed to react to their own bodies. Instead of focusing on that little belly, I assumed that the majority of children would rather focus on the sequins on the leotard or the way the fluffy tutu bounced up and down while dancing. I did not have a chance to pay attention to the tiny details as I was critiquing my own self through a microscope. It was how I learned.

I started learning to critique myself about 16 years ago, when I remember judging myself. I am now 19 years old and a sophomore in college, although a lot of the time, I feel like I am still that child facing herself in the glass door.

"Erin? Are you okay?" the young therapist asked as

my mind drifted off and my eyes stared into space.

"Uhh…oh, yeah. Yeah, I'm fine." I scribbled down gibberish on the paper to make it seem as though I was actually working. I did not need to give an answer to the question, any way. I had already received the worksheet before and my answers had not changed. If I was asked to give my opinion, I could easily remember what I wrote last time. Luckily, the clock soon turned to 8:00 and it was time for us to leave for the day. We all ran to the door and waited for one of the nurses to swipe her ID badge to let us free in the outside world.

The outside world was a much more dangerous place than the locked quarters of which we were confined, but we felt liberated once we stepped past the barrier marking the safe place and the world beyond our bubble. Most of us did not know how to survive in the more dangerous environment. Whether by choice or force, we have had to trust that the confined, safe environment would be a place where we could learn and grow, eventually giving us the strength to know how to survive.

"Bye, guys! See you tomorrow." I shouted, as I walked to my car and began the drive home. Driving was my time to think to myself, to have alone time, or to jam out to loud music if I wanted to lift my spirits.

Within a half an hour, I made it home, and was prepared for the daily questions about my day. I opened the door and soon heard the automatic greeting my parents had grown to love: "So, how'd it go?"

I was never quite sure how to answer the question, as I was not convinced it was something they really cared to hear. My parents were not the type of people who asked questions to know more about someone's day, and they only started asking me because it was mentioned in therapy as a tip in order to be more helpful. I was sure they wanted to be more helpful, but sometimes it was annoying to be asked to explain the day when all I wanted was to relax and rot my brain in front of the television after hours of thinking.

My answer to them: "Fine." Usually, that answer satisfied them, but I knew I could not use that answer for the rest of my life. Eventually, they would learn that I am not "fine" every day, and that by saying "fine" was just another way of saying "I don't really feel like talking."

Emotions in our house were rarely talked about. For whatever reason, our emotions and feelings were swept under the rug and were magically dealt with, without us ever explaining them or rationalizing thoughts. I assumed that it worked like this in every household so I never questioned it. My dad was brought up to be the macho man, to take care of the wife and kids, to bring home the bacon and suck things up when things got rough. My mom was raised in a similar fashion in terms of emotions, in that they were just emotions and they did not really need to be talked about. Talking things out was not necessary then and it was not necessary now.

"I'm going upstairs."

"What about your snack?" asked my mom.

Having a snack every night was a new routine for me. I did not like the routine because it was a foreign experience, something I was not used to, nor was it something I enjoyed.

For such a long time, I got away with eating very little throughout the day. My weight dropped and my mind became a mass of crazy thoughts that made no sense any more. My brain was not functioning properly and I am not sure how I was able to complete school projects while running on empty. I did not want to eat, yet I knew that eating would be the only way out of the fog that was my world. When my body was starved, the world around me seemed so distant and so unreal. The real world became the outside world of which we are all so afraid. Even though the fogginess clouded everything in sight and my body was too tired to do much else but sleep, the fear was still there, making its way closer and closer every passing day.

I had never been good at dealing with the problems of life, even from a very young age. The thoughts and emotions that came from my head sometimes frightened me, yet I kept them to myself and never said a word. Anxiety became a big part of my every day routine. I mistakenly thought that every eight year old must have felt that sense of impending doom, that one day everything would fall apart and the world would end. I did not recognize that others my age were not worried about the sky falling. They were not anxious about the test coming up in three weeks. The forgotten homework was not a big deal to them.

Anxiety was something that I had never been able to shake, and so started the endless battle of trying to rid myself from it. The emotion of anxiety was not something I would wish upon any one, not even my worst enemy. My weapon of choice to fight the battle was food.

Little did I know, that choice would not only make

that battle worse, but it would also start a new war within myself.

I

IT'S NOT HARD TO GET SUCKED IN

I stepped toward my instrument of obsession as my heart pounded faster, the beating echoing in my ears. The anxiety I felt was nothing new but I had never been able to get used to the feeling. The overwhelming sense of failure and defeat washed over me even before I could know whether or not those feelings were even legitimate. Perspiration began to collect on my palms and my heart rate increased even more. I took a deep breath and made the final step onto the platform. My hands shook nervously as I carefully slid the weights back and forth on the scaled rod. It was a balancing act, not only literally, but my sanity was increasingly becoming something less than stable. The arrow came to a stop and pointed out the result I was so anxiously awaiting.

I lost weight. Yes, I lost weight! A smile appeared from my terrified grin and I pumped my fists in the air in excitement. My pulse quickly slowed down to normal and my racing thoughts disappeared, waiting for the next chance to haunt. I was relieved, at least for the moment. In that moment, I was content and satisfied with the outcome of my daily test, but it did not always work out for the better.

The scale had become my monster's tool. Instead of an angry, fear hunting creature under a child's bed, what I feared most was an inanimate object used to weigh people and things. There was nothing scary about the exterior; it was only one big piece of metal with a few mechanical parts. There was nothing fancy about it, as it was designed only to do its job. But what that monster dragged out from within me was scarier than any demon I could imagine.

Even though I was terrified of the monster, I was also obsessively attracted to it. I chose to let its decisions rule me and my decisions. Based on what it told me, I could have either an amazing day, or a horrible day, despite the actual events that were occurring. I am not sure where, when, or how the fixation started, but what I do know is that once the monster had its grip on me, it felt nearly impossible to free myself from the lies and deceit.

Somehow, a simple tool such as the scale became the

tool that dictated emotions and reasoning, something I was never very good at, any way. The scale became my decision maker. There was only one thing that needed to be remembered: Losing weight will make me happy. That is it, no ifs, ands, or buts. It replayed in my mind over and over again like a broken record. If I achieved that, my life would play out as I had always wanted. Losing weight would make me confident and give me the courage that I lacked before. Losing weight would make life so much easier and I would not need to question anything ever again. I would be given the answers to life.

At least, that is what the monster had promised me.

It crept into my life ever so slowly, seemingly innocent and non-threatening, appearing in disguise as my New Year's Resolution. I held my arms wide open and welcomed this new presence into my life. Finally, I thought, I would be able to make myself happy. I had found the answer! I did not have anything to lose and I was willing to give up everything. I tossed my better judgment aside and chose to put my faith in the new-found idea. The promises sounded so tempting and I could not look away. I had found my best friend, but that best friend was wearing two faces. I failed to see the evil side and mistakenly agreed to play the game. I signed my life away and from then on, my actions would be controlled by some other force, a force much more powerful than my own rationale and myself.

First came the test of my willpower. Would I be able to control my food intake or would I succumb to my own gluttonous desires?

Food was much harder to deny than I imagined. I

thought that if I set my mind to the task, it would be easy. It was not. There was no easy way of fighting off that hunger sensation other than getting used to it, or by giving my body what it wanted. As my stomach would growl and moan, my mind reacted and yelled back. My logical self knew that I needed fuel in order to have enough energy to get through the day, yet my mind and the monster took over the show. When it came to the monster, it always won. The monster was the boss.

No matter how hungry I became, my mind shouted back, telling my stomach to stay quiet and explaining to me that I really was not hungry. I was convinced that the hunger pangs were only temporary and food was not necessary in my goal to become happy. In order to achieve that ultimate goal, I had to lose the weight.

The human body is very skilled at knowing when something just is not right. A body infected with an airborne virus brings on a cough. An overworked body produces sweat in order for it to cool itself down. A hungry body is no different, as it repeatedly shouts at its owner to satisfy it with nutrition and calories. When the body is hungry for food, the body lets it be known. The sensation of an empty stomach begging for food became addicting once I got over the pain and discomfort. The pain was no longer painful. Emptiness meant that very little or no calories had been consumed, and my flatter stomach made me feel thinner, even if it was all in my head. Sometimes it felt as though tiny little people were inside of me, pushing and pulling at my insides, whispering to me to take a bite of food, making it harder and harder for me to ignore the hunger. I thought of it as a test, another test that I could easily pass in order to keep myself on the path to happiness. If I could keep going, I would surely feel differently about myself soon, right?

It did not take very long for me to start changing my habits. Normally, before my new-found challenge, I never looked at nutrition labels on packages and I did not really care about how many calories I was eating at every meal. I had soon become an expert at calorie counting. I was not able to eat until I examined the labels. Any food that came into view, I could rattle off its calorie count without hesitation. I was quite proud of my unique feat; I thought that not many other people knew as much as I did.

My meals were slowly getting smaller and smaller, yet I hid the fact quite well so that no one noticed what I was doing. By eliminating items one by one, the change was not drastic and I was never questioned as to why I was eating less. I became high on my accomplishments. I thought that maybe I would be able to push myself even further than I had ever thought possible. My memory was performing surprisingly well, considering the amount of food I was putting into my body, and I could easily list what I had eaten for an entire week. Weight and food became more important to me than anything.

I compare my obsession to that of a drug addict. I am not and have never been a drug addict, but I can only assume that it is the same mentality. The high I got from my hunger was equivalent to the high induced by cocaine. Even without much fuel, I was able to perform very well in class. Instead of being tired, my adrenaline rushed through my veins because of my excitement. I was super-human and did not need calories like other people.

After a while, hunger became my normal state of being. I was succeeding so far in achieving my goal. I had lost a few pounds, and I thought to myself, why not lose a few more? A few pounds would solidify the happiness I was looking for and it gave me another little challenge to keep pushing myself.

Realistically, before I even started dropping pounds, my body did not necessarily need to lose any weight at all. I had always been an athlete and so my body was fit and far from overweight. But my body did not look like those in the magazines, either. Instead of muscular, athletic builds, I noticed that the most popular girls in magazines, movies, and television were very thin. They had no muscles like I did. They looked frail and delicate, yet also weak. Their weakness somehow drew me in and I frequently wished I could look like them. I knew that most women in the real world looked nothing like the famous celebrities, but their image seemed almost magical and perfect. Perfect. They seemed perfect. I daydreamed of the day when I would look like them and be just as flawless.

I had fallen victim to society's endless portrayal of the "All American Woman." This "All American Woman" could do everything she put her mind to, all while looking impeccable and with a smile on her face. She made no mistakes and she knew all of the right answers. Her body matched her personality, a compatible companion to the mind of the woman every girl wanted to be. Only, the "All American Woman" was an imaginary character, pretending to be like the typical housewife, student, and daughter every one saw walking the streets. I strived to become the character I saw every day, the character that was shoved in my face for entertainment and brainwashing. My life would be problem free once I was that woman, I thought.

2

CRACKS IN THE LIES

It seems as though I've gotten a job at Camp Barnes, meaning I will be away for a full eight weeks starting next Tuesday. Orientation/training week is Tuesday through Friday, and then the campers come on Sunday....every Sunday through Friday. I'm very anxious about making friends and meeting people, but I assume they will all be nice. I'm assuming I'll make friends with at least one of the other girls. I'm also nervous about being away for so long. Not because I'll miss home, but because of eating *stuations. At home, I am in complete control. I don't know what to expect there.*

As my obsessions grew stronger and stronger through the year, my mind now had to focus on my new job as a camp counselor at a sleep away camp for young children. My weight and food had to be something to put on the back burner for the duration of the summer, only I was not quite sure how to make that happen. I hoped that the ever-so-present monster in my head would quiet itself while I worked with children. Adding children into the mix changed situations entirely and I was not sure how I would be able to stay true to my duties as a counselor and keep track of my growing fascination of toying with my body.

Since my new found challenge had started taking up most of my time, mostly mentally, I failed to notice that I isolated myself from my family and friends. Because I was working at a camp for the summer, I was no longer isolated. I had to function in the real world with real people, not some imaginary world within my mind. I was living with 12 other girls in one huge room, something I was definitely not used to. Being an only child allowed me to have my own room. I liked having my own space and I was safe and comfortable being alone while at home or at college. Interacting with others seemed like a weird ritual to me since I had not done it very much in quite a long time.

Sticking out from the crowd was always something I worried about. With every move I made, I was conscious of my actions and how others would perceive me. Being stuck in a group of 23 of my peers was not my idea of a good time. I had no idea how I would get through the summer. My distorted thinking told me that I was different from everyone else and no one understood who I was or what I was about. The mind plays dirty tricks on those who lack confidence and my mind let me know that I was not as good as the others.

The anxiety overwhelmed me and I immediately felt out of place. I asked myself, how was everyone else able to socialize and be comfortable with being themselves? Apparently, I had missed the socialization class in life. I was probably too busy thinking of the calories in my organic granola bar. Already shy from a young age, my apprehension to speak to others must have been obvious to everyone else. In a room full of people, I was still alone. To make matters worse, one of the first activities we had together was dinner. I silently moaned to myself while everyone else was thrilled at the thought of scoring some free food. Eating in front of others was especially hard for me.

"Hi, I'm Amber! What's your name?" A petite girl stood next to me in line as we waited for the food to be set out.

"Oh, hi. I'm Erin." I smiled politely and had no idea what to say next. Luckily, she had an outgoing personality that made things easier for me.

"Cool. Where are you from? I came all the way from Arizona, just got in today."

"I don't live far from here. Just outside of D.C." I wondered if she was truly interested or if she was just being nice and making conversation.

Our dinner soon appeared and everyone quickly rushed to the table to get first picks. I heard a few guys yell out a few cheers and all were excited but me. I dreaded eating meals, much less meals with others sitting around, eating at the same time. I feared that people would stare and judge me based on my food choices. I was horrified at the thought of someone whispering to another, telling them how fat I was or how much weight I would gain from eating a certain food.

As I stepped up to the buffet table, my fear turned into panic. The dinner: fried chicken with mashed potatoes, green beans, and biscuits. There was absolutely no way I was going to eat that chicken. Racing thoughts took over my brain, racing thoughts of calories and fat and the oil that was used to fry that chicken. I could picture the fat dripping from the crispy skin, the butter soaking through the layers of the biscuit. Green beans were usually okay in my book, but did the cook add anything to them? What if butter was added to them, too? How much butter was thrown into the mashed potatoes? What was I supposed to eat?

I excused myself and ran to the bathroom. My palms met my face and I began sobbing, tears freely flowing from my eyes. I did not know how I was going to deal with meals every day. This was just the beginning. There were no nutrition labels to read before I ate, and at home, I carefully calculated every calorie before I took the first bite. I was not going to be able to know my caloric intake for meals. I also had no scale to track my progress.

The door swung open and Amber walked over to me.

"Are you okay?"

"Yeah. Something's in my eye." I was great at lying when it came to my emotions. No one ever knew if I was sad. I had always figured that I could be dying of a gunshot wound and I would still be able to reassure everyone around that I really was fine.

I wiped the tears from my cheeks with a rough paper towel and hesitantly returned to the buffet table with Amber. A deep breath entered my lungs as I dipped the spoon into the first dish.

My dinner that night consisted of a mound of green beans and a spoonful of mashed potatoes. Cleverness struck and I told everyone else that I ate before I came to camp that day. The only problem was that excuse would not work any longer.

I managed to fool everyone again during breakfast the next morning. My excuse? "I don't really eat breakfast." The majority of the other girls did not eat breakfast all too often, either. The plan for the day was to get to know each other a little better and then go off on a hike through the woods. I was not too keen on getting to know everyone better, just because of the awkwardness, but I was looking forward to the hike. It meant that I would get some exercise and burn a few calories. I was not really one to seek out exercise for the fun of it, but I also was not going to turn down an opportunity.

I laced up my tennis shoes nice and tight and joined my fellow co-workers at the start of the hiking trail. Some of the boys had already trekked through the woods to satisfy their curiosity, but for most of us, it was our first time.

The gravel that marked the beginning of the trail

slipped under the soles of my shoes. We walked quite a bit and landed at a campsite that was used by campers throughout the summer. Sleeping outside was another thing I was not looking forward to doing, but I figured that this would be a summer to test my comfort level. It had already been tested with something as simple as food. After resting at the campsite for a while, gulping down water in order to stay hydrated, we continued down a steep incline of a sloped walkway. We crossed a beautiful bridge, which was built over a narrow stream. I stepped down from the wooden structure and my eyes grew wider as I saw what was ahead.

"We're climbing that??" My voice trembled as I asked another girl, Danielle.

"Yep! Pretty cool, huh?"

I was not thrilled with the idea of climbing a mountain of a hill that was supposedly a part of a nature trail. The incline was something that would intimidate the most advanced hikers. Fallen trees blocked parts of the passage where we were to cross. Large rocks were spotted throughout, as well. I did not feel ready to continue on this challenge, yet there was no other way to get back to camp. I had to go forward and follow everyone else.

As I started moving up the hill, I quickly grew winded and it became harder and harder for me to breathe. Climbing such a hill was a workout, but it should not have been as hard as it was for me, being only 19. The others did not seem to have the same problem. Their legs were burning from the intensity but they were not panting, nor did they look scared as if something was wrong. By the time we got halfway up the hill, I had to stop and take a break for a few minutes. My heart was pounding so much that I thought I saw my shirt rise up and down with the beat. Sweat was starting to drip down my face as my body was not used to such a hard task. I sucked it up and continued to move.

Slowly, I made it to the top of the hike, thrilled that I did not pass out on the way. But just as I was celebrating my success, my vision became darkened and my head was spinning. In order to control the sensations, I had to crouch down on the ground while pretending everything was okay. I did not want anyone to know how horrible I was really feeling. Randy, a certified personal trainer, suggested that everyone check their pulse to make sure our hearts were working properly. I placed my fingers on the side of my neck and counted for 30 seconds, then doubled that number to figure out my pulse rate. It was well above what would be considered normal for someone my age, only I told everyone else that I was completely fine.

I slowly stood up after the tiny black dots cleared from my vision and took a sip of water. For a minute, I wondered why it was so hard for me to complete an exercise that was relatively easy for others my age. The answer was so obvious but I did not think it would make such an impact. Of course, my eating, or lack thereof, was starting to be apparent to my body. My body started battling with my mind. It was not happy at what I was doing. My body had been handling things well up until that point. But for the moment, I chose to ignore what it was physically telling me. I chose to listen to my mind instead.

A few days later, the kids arrived at camp ready to run around day after day and have fun. I was excited since I had always loved working with children. The innocence of those who do not know the truth of the world was amazing to see. I missed that innocence of childhood when the biggest problem in life was picking out the color of a shirt to wear that day.

All 24 counselors were separated into groups of four, six counselors together, three boys and three girls. I was placed with the youngest group of kids, my favorite. I assumed that eating with the young kids would be an easy task and they would never pick up on my weird eating habits. They would not know that how I was eating was harmful to my body. They were not that smart, were they?

I thought wrong. They were only nine, but they were fully aware that what I was doing was not normal.

One morning after I made sure that my table of kids had all of their food, I sat down in my chair at the head of the table. What sat in front of me was barely a snack: a mini box of Froot Loops with no milk and a cup of coffee. What was worse was my habit of eating the sugary cereal. Unknowingly, I picked out each piece of cereal one by one. Not only that, I categorized them by color and ate them in a specific order. I was very meticulous and failed to notice the nine year old staring at my ritual.

"Why do you eat your cereal like that?"

Her question startled me. I was not expecting the children to pick up on my obsessive symptoms.

"Like what?" I played dumb as if I had no idea what she was talking about.

"You eat them in order! Why? Why do you eat so little? Are you trying to lose weight or something?" Her puzzled look concerned me. I realized that I did not want to influence the children in any negative ways.

"Oh, I didn't even notice!" I lied and continued to eat my cereal, making sure to eat them at random. She seemed convinced of my answer but came back with another statement.

"You don't need to lose weight, you know! You're skinny."

How a nine-year-old girl would even know about weight loss surprised me, until I thought back to when I was that age. I knew about weight loss much earlier. It has become weaved into our culture and children have learned about weight loss at a very young age.

The days at camp seemed to drag on forever. Because of the heat of summer and the screaming kids, I was becoming very exhausted. I promised myself that I could stick to my strict eating habits, no matter what was thrown my way. I was sticking to my plan but it seemed to be making me miserable. Many people hate being miserable, however, being miserable only reminded me that I was staying on the path. It had become my path of safety, my path of control when things seemed too overwhelming. I was starting to think that maybe I was going to need to choose between that path and another path in order to stay working. The other path would be to throw my food rules out of the window and hope that I would not gain any weight over the summer. I was not too sure about that option. How was I supposed to change my direction and change my ways? I was so used to relying on my obsessions for comfort. When kids were loud in the dining hall, I could focus my attention on the number of peas on my plate. If I felt disgusting and overweight, I could focus on my hunger pangs and that let me know I was safe.

In my logical mind, I knew that sticking it out at camp would be the better option, but my other half disagreed. I wanted to stick to my habits and goals and that would be impossible to do if I stayed there working. I was quickly losing energy and I would not make it through the rest of the summer. Ultimately, I decided to leave the kids and my fellow co-workers in order to stay on track. Admittedly, I felt guilty for quitting and backing out on my promise, but my promise to myself was much more important. I let my boss know that I would be leaving for personal reasons. He did not ask any questions, which relieved me.

Instead of telling everyone the truth and saying goodbye in person, I left a note for the whole group to read. I failed to mention to anyone why I was truly leaving because I do not think anyone would believe that it was a valid reason. Leaving out the truth was my best bet and it saved me from any humiliation or questions. I just wanted to leave and be on my way, my way back to striving for excellence and perfection by way of weight, calories, and food. I would have more time to think and obsess, and my body would be able to regain its strength lost from the harsh regime during camp.

There was no turning around again; I only saw a "One Way" sign ahead, pointing to the path of happiness and confidence. I saw the obstacles in the way but I continued on any way. The obstacles ahead did not scare me one bit.

3

THE BODY
FIGHTS BACK

What a fun week. Lots of sickness, but at least I did not have to put up with the bratty campers. This morning I sound like a man since my throat is rough and hurts a bit. My body is on a very different clock now, since I'm used to waking up early at camp every day. I thought I'd sleep in a little later since I'm at home, but I woke up at 8:45. That's actually late considering I usually wake up at 6:45 every day, but still. Waking up early has its benefits *though. I love the peacefulness of night time, but waking up early makes me feel like I'm living my day to the fullest.*

Up until the time my body started reacting to the pressure I had placed upon it, I thought that I was invincible and that nothing would be able to hurt me. My body did not need food like everyone else, my body could function just fine with the little calories I was eating, I thought. I still was not fully convinced that what I was doing was harming my body, but unfortunately, my body disagreed. When I got back home after returning from camp, my body sighed with relief.

And then crashed.

At first, I thought that maybe I was just catching a summer cold, since many people I came in contact with had the virus. I did not pay much attention to it until I got out of bed the day after I returned home. When I stood up, the floor shook and my head spun. My world was completely unstable and I had to sit back down in order to keep myself from falling over. I rested my head in my hands and I heard my heart beat through my skull. I was not feeling so well. I yelled to my mom and asked her to bring me the thermometer so I could take my temperature. I was not one to use the thermometer too often, one because I was never sick, but I always sucked it up even when I did have a fever.

"Here you go." She placed her hand on my head to see if I felt warm. "Hmm. You feel fine to me."

I stuck the thermometer into my ear and waited for the beep. It read 98.7. The reading confused me a bit since I was starting to feel very sick but I dismissed it and decided to lie down.

"Do you want anything?"

"No, I'm fine. I'm just gonna go to bed."

As soon as my head hit the pillow and my eyes shut, I was out and had entered dreamland.

Not only had food taken over my mind while I was awake, it had started to take over my dreams, as well. The same dream kept coming back to me, night after night. In the dream, it seemed like any other day. I woke up, brushed my teeth, got dressed, everything that is routine for any person in the world. But instead of skipping breakfast like I would normally do in real life, I ate a mountain of food and binged until my stomach ached and I could not move from the kitchen chair. Food was haunting me through my dreams just the same way it was haunting me while I was awake. Drifting out of sleep and back into the real world, my heart raced and I panicked at the thought of inhaling so much food at once. I could not believe that something so simple could keep me so terrified.

I glanced at the clock and noticed that eight hours had passed since I first rested my head on my pillow. Confused, I looked at my watch to make sure the time was correct. I started to question the validity of my sight since I had just woken up, but I soon realized that I had, in fact, slept for eight hours straight. I first fell asleep during the early afternoon and now it was time to head back to sleep again.

My mom was surely still awake so I started my journey downstairs to find her.

"You're awake!" She did not seem too concerned

about the amount of time I spent in bed.

"Why'd you let me sleep so long?? I'll never be able to go to sleep tonight."

"Yes, you will. You need your rest when you're sick."

My mouth was dry and sticky so I went to fetch a glass of water. I gulped down the liquid in record time and my thirst was quenched for the time being.

She also suggested that I grab a snack while I was in the kitchen.

"You're looking really thin. Have you lost weight?"

I shrugged my shoulders and declined to answer. Of course, I knew I had lost weight, quite a bit of it, but I was not going to admit it. If I admitted it, I would for sure be asked questions about why. My weight was significantly lower than it was at the beginning of the year and I was surprised at why more people had not asked or commented on how different I looked. My clothes were hanging off my body, forcing me to wear belts and drown in oversized shirts. I could feel my hipbones through my jeans and as I ran my hand up my spine, I could feel each vertebra through my shirt. These signs showed me that what I was doing to myself was working. I wanted to see those bones and even though I was starting to look like a malnourished prisoner, I appreciated the fact that I had accomplished something.

I chose not to get a snack as my mom suggested. Hunger was not a problem and I did not think a snack was necessary, any way. It was only extra calories. Instead, I went back to my room to sleep. The fatigue was still apparent as my body laid on my bed, even though I slept the day away. I closed my eyes and welcomed the peaceful darkness of slumber.

The next morning, I was awoken by my mom shoving a plate of scrambled eggs and bacon in my face.

"Good morning! You have to be hungry. Eat this, I made it for you."

I grabbed the plate and smiled, pretending to be thankful, secretly disgusted on the inside. I used to enjoy the nice breakfasts my mom cooked for me.

"Thanks."

A genius plan entered my head when my mom left the room. My plan? I decided to dump my breakfast down the toilet, leaving only a few bites and crumbs on the plate, leaving others to think that I had eaten the meal. I had never been a liar or liked to deceive any one, but now as I was diving into the world of obsession, lying came easily to me. It was not hard to lie about the food I had supposedly eaten or how I was really feeling. As long as the outcome was in my favor, everything was fine. The guilt I felt was only a minor consequence.

About an hour after I flushed the meal down the toilet, I was informed that I would be going to the doctor's office that afternoon. My mom called my doctor earlier in the day and asked to schedule an appointment. She was worried about my excessive sleeping and wanted to make sure there was not something seriously wrong with me. I had seen the same doctor for years and she would have to notice the shift in my weight, but I wondered if she would say anything to me about it. To make sure, before I left to see the doctor, I dropped a bag of pennies in each of my pants pockets. The pennies would ensure I would weight a little bit more on the scale, but not so much that it would be obvious.

I had never liked going to the see the doctor, even for routine check-ups every year. Even though doctors see many different bodies of all different shapes and sizes, from a very young age I was self-conscious about my body. Before every appointment, I would beg my mom to cancel the appointment. After all, I was never sick and there was nothing wrong with me. Only, she insisted I go. She was a responsible mom, and I needed my shots and vaccinations. I had never been comfortable being around people while I was naked, even slightly showing skin. In middle school when I needed to change in the locker room for gym class, I would always make sure I was hidden underneath my clothes so that no one could look at me. The other girls were probably self-conscious, as well, but they did not show their fear.

The worst part about seeing the doctor was sitting on the examination table waiting for my body to be viewed. I always tried to suck in my stomach and sit up straight because I had to look my best. And as much as I knew that looking at the intimate parts of the body was routine, it made me very insecure when the doctor would have to look. I was not even comfortable viewing my own body and I did not want any one else to see, either.

When I arrived at the doctor's office, I was immediately placed in the sick room to the side, just in case I had the flu so I would not infect other healthy patients. The television in the room was showing "Finding Nemo," a movie I had only seen parts of while sitting around at camp. The other kids did not pay attention to the animated fish and were instead building a castle with the wooden blocks. After about a half hour of painfully waiting, I was called back into the examination room.

"Hi, Erin. I am going to ask you to put on this gown, and then I will be back in a minute to take a few simple tests before the doctor comes in. Ok?"

"Ok...thanks." It slipped my mind that I would have to change into a gown before I was weighed. There were no pockets in the gown for my bags of pennies. Where would I hide them? I was out of luck; there was no way to fool the doctor today. I changed into the uncomfortable paper gown and waited for the nurse to come back into the room. Disappointed, I tried to think of an excuse to tell the doctor in case she asked why I lost weight. A few things came to mind:

- I exercised a lot this summer, unintentionally. (*Not totally false.*)
- I was not really trying to lose weight but it just happened. (*Not true.*)
- I have been starving myself. (*True, but there was no way I would come clean.*)

The nurse came back into the room and we headed out to the hallway where the scale was sitting. It was a much more elaborate scale than the one at my house and I wondered if the numbers would be the same.

"Ok, stand up straight for me."

I already knew how to take a proper weight. I had been stepping on the scale every day, multiple times per day, for months now. The machine beeped and let the nurse know the number to write down on my chart. She compared the number with the one from my last visit.

"You've lost weight. Good for you!"

Ha! She congratulated me on losing weight! Maybe if she did not notice anything, then the doctor would not notice anything, either. We walked back into the exam room so she could take my temperature and blood pressure. The temperature gauge poked my ear and the blood pressure cuff was pumping my arm at the same time. The first blood pressure attempt did not work so the nurse had to take it again.

"Your temperature is a little low. Let's see how your pressure is...." We waited for a moment until the result showed on the screen. "So is your blood pressure. No wonder you don't feel well." She placed the instruments back where they belonged and made her way out the door. "I'll go get the doctor, she should be with you in a few minutes."

My blood pressure had always been normal and my temperature was never lower than the norm, either. The fact that both were unusually low concerned me for a second, but I chalked it up to being sick. I figured that when someone was ill, the body would try all sorts of tricks in order to fight off the enemy.

My eyes wandered around the room and I got lost in the paintings on the walls. There were pictures of serene mountains from a far away land, some place I wished I could travel. Interrupting my thoughts, the doctor came in to greet me.

"Hello, Erin. It's been a while since I've seen you!"

She performed a routine exam and asked me the basic questions that were asked at every doctor's visit. Then she began talking about something I hoped she would not mention: my weight.

"I've noticed you've lost a significant amount of weight since I last saw you. Now, I know you have grown up a bit and probably lost your baby fat, but I am a bit concerned about the dramatic change. What's going on?"

I stared at her with a blank expression on my face. I froze in fear and did not know how to answer her. The excuses that I thought of only a few minutes before had escaped my brain and I was left with a blank slate. I could both lie and pretend like I had become so good at, or I could tell the truth and be the honest girl I had always been.

"Ummm...." My voice trailed off and my stare moved down to the floor. My shoulders shrugged in response.

"I am worried that you have possibly done this to yourself. Your tests and weight show that you are severely dehydrated. Dehydration is not uncommon, but with your symptoms and weight loss, I am concerned that this is something more serious than a common cold or fatigue." She looked worried and she had connected the puzzle pieces together without me saying a word.

"I don't drink that much." A reason left my mouth so that I was not admitting or denying anything.

"Well, I can see that. But I want you to get some tests so you can see how your body is holding up, ok?" She turned around to a panel of handouts and grabbed a brochure. "Also, I am not accusing you of anything, but take a look at this. Since you are 19, I am not allowed to tell your parents anything and your information is confidential. Your health is your responsibility now."

A blue pamphlet was handed in my direction with a sad looking teenager on the front. The title read, "Eating Disorders: How to Know When to Get Help"

Eating disorders? My doctor thought I had an eating disorder? I did not look like those dying anorexic girls I had seen on television and I did not throw up my food, so I was not bulimic. I was just a little obsessed, that was all. And even though I lost weight, I was still not very underweight. I did not have an eating disorder! I thanked her for the information, though.

"You're sick from dehydration. You are going to need to drink plenty of fluids and rest for the next few days. Proper meals are essential, too. Do not strain yourself. And no exercise. Alright?"

I agreed. I was sure that I was sick, not just dehydrated, but I accepted her diagnosis. After all, she was the doctor. I picked up my clothes from the chair, got dressed, and headed out to the waiting room to meet my mom.

"Let's go." I said.

"Is everything ok? What's wrong?"

"I just need to drink more fluids, that's all. I must have overworked while I was at camp. I just need to take it easy for a few days." I told my mom nothing about the doctor's comments and I hid the pamphlet on eating disorders in my bag. My mind was spinning and I began to doubt myself for the first time.

But I really did not have an eating disorder, did I?

4

TEST ANXIETY

The next day, I traveled to the outpatient medical clinic near my home in order to complete some tests my doctor wanted me to have done. I held in my hand two white prescription sheets, one for blood work and one for a bone density scan. I decided to get my blood work out of the way first since I knew what to expect. I entered the office and noticed that I was the only patient in the waiting room. The receptionist called me to the desk straight away and asked me for my information and prescription.

"You're here for a routine test? A complete blood

test?" She wore dark blue scrubs and looked as though she had not slept much the night before. I did not think being nice was one of her strong suits.

"Yes. I think so." I was not sure what a complete blood test entailed and I only knew that I was there for a blood test. The doctor never told me which one.

"Take a seat, it won't be long."

I turned around to find a chair and spotted the television in the corner of the room. Coincidentally, "Finding Nemo" was playing at this office, as well. I let out a giggle and half-questioned whether or not somebody was playing a joke on me. As I grabbed the "People" magazine sitting next to my chair, I heard a soft voice call my name.

"Erin? You can come back."

I followed the woman in white to a tiny room in the back of the suite. There were colored balloons plastered on the wall to keep children's eyes occupied as they waited. The radio was set on a pop music radio station and I started to relax in the stiff chair.

"Which arm?" I held up my right arm and placed it on the armrest assuming that it would be a better target to give blood. I only had blood drawn a few times before and I remembered that my left arm had given the nurses trouble for some reason. The nurse tied the elastic band around my bicep and rubbed a wet cotton pad where she was going to prick me. The alcohol from the cotton cooled my arm. I clenched my fist together and patiently waited for the jab of the needle.

"Ready?" She took a breath and carefully injected the needle into my vein. I only felt a prick and it was pretty painless. "Hmm..."

Whenever I heard any health professionals questioning what they had done, I started to panic. I assumed that because they do procedures numerous times, nothing could go wrong.

"What's wrong?" I asked, starting to get worried.

"I'm not getting a flash. Your blood isn't coming up into the vial. Let me try again."

Just what I wanted, another stabbing with the needle, but it had to be done. She repeated the process and stuck the sharp stick into my arm once more. Still, nothing happened.

"Jane, could you come over here for a minute? I'm not getting a flash."

Another nurse walked over to us and grabbed the needle from the woman's hand. It was still planted in my arm but Jane tried to maneuver the tip in different directions to get a blood flow.

"Ouch." I groaned. That hurt much worse than the initial stab.

"Nope, not getting anything. Try the hand with the butterfly needle."

My mom told me previously about her experience with a needle stuck into her hand. She informed me that it stung worse than the arm. Of course, my arm had to be the one in a million that did not work properly.

The nurse grabbed a different, smaller needle and poked into the top of my hand. Finally, my blood started dripping out into the vial. I thanked God in my head so I would not have to face yet another prick. She filled two vials with my blood and I watched as the dark red liquid streamed into the transparent tube.

Suddenly, I started feeling lightheaded and my stomach flipped inside out. A tingly feeling entered my throat and I felt as though I was going to throw up.

"I don't feel well. I think I might vomit."

Luckily, they got all the blood that was needed by that point. The nurse then took the needle out from my hand, put a bandage over the tiny hole, and pointed me in the direction of the bathroom.

My feet quickly took me to the pure white room across the hall. I crouched down in front of the toilet and rested my arms on the cold porcelain seat. The germs would have normally freaked me out but I felt too sick to pay attention at that moment. In silence, I waited for my stomach to do its duty and my body to reject whatever was inside. Nothing ever came up, much to my relief. Tiny black dots appeared in my vision so I stayed stooped down with my head rested on my hands. The nurse knocked on the door to ask if I was okay.

"Yeah, I'm fine. Thanks." I waited a few minutes before I stood up, until my vision was clear again. My face reflected back at me in the mirror hanging on the wall. My skin was pale and I did not look very well. The cool water from the sink ran down my face as I tried to gather myself. My stomach was not feeling completely better but I did not feel the need to throw up anymore.

"I'm ok." As I exited, I smiled at the nurses to make sure they knew I was all right.

"Alright, hon. You're all done here, you can leave. Have a good day!"

I grabbed my bag that was sitting on the seat next to me and walked out of the office.

One appointment down, one to go. The next test I needed to go to was in the very next building so I decided to walk instead of moving my car from one parking lot to another.

At first, I thought I was in the wrong building. All around me were older men and women, no one my age was to be seen. I approached the receptionist and asked if I was in the right place. Yes, I was, I was at the right place. I thought it was a bit odd but I did not think much of it. The middle-aged woman handed me the paperwork to fill out and directed me to the waiting room chairs.

The cushy chairs were relaxing, much better than the chairs at the last place. But this office did not have a television. I grabbed the pen and started to fill out the paperwork. One of the questions was if I was going through menopause or if I had already gone through menopause. I wondered again, why this center was so focused on older patients, and then the answer came to me.

I was there to get a bone density scan. Healthy 19 year old's do not usually need to get a bone density scan because healthy 19 year old's do not need to worry about their bones. Usually, bone problems were more likely to occur in older women who had already gone through menopause. I was certain that my bones were still fine and that my doctor wanted the test done just to make sure. My weird food rituals and calorie counting had only been going on since the beginning of the year, not a long time. It was not enough time to do any damage, I thought.

I autographed the bottom of the paperwork and patiently waited to be called back into the exam room. Since I had never had a bone scan performed, I had no idea what to expect. Anxiety started to set in but just as it started to escalate, a friendly, young brunette called my name to come back to the room.

"Hi, Erin, I'm Rebecca. This won't take long at all." She led me down a narrow hallway, past a few x-ray rooms, and into a changing cubicle. "Here's a gown. Take everything off but your underwear and I'll come and get you in a few minutes."

I was stuck in a tiny space with a full-length mirror straight ahead. My clothes quickly came off and I caught myself looking at my body, nitpicking every inch, criticizing my extra fat, noticing all of the imperfections. I hated looking at my body but when I started criticizing, time passed extraordinarily fast and I forgot about everything else in the world. Since I dove into the world of body hatred, I had not noticed that Rebecca came back.

"Are you ready?"

I threw on the gown and quickly tied the strings together. It was oversized and too big to tie together properly, leaving part of my back exposed. Rebecca led me back down the hall and into a small room containing a few machines I had never seen before.

"Ok, sweetie, I need you to lay down right here."

She pointed to the platform on a big x-ray machine. I laid down and rested my head on the stiff pillow that was provided. Rebecca carefully lifted up my legs and placed them on top of a triangular foam pillow, leaving my knees bent and a bit uncomfortable.

"Just hold still, this won't take long."

I took a deep breath to relax and counted the loud clicks that radiated from the machine. My body held still but I was worried about moving, even if it was only from breathing. The first set of x-rays finished and started again soon after, moving above my hip, then finally to the bottom of my spine.

The test was painless and was just like any other x-ray I have ever gotten; although, I did wonder how much radiation I had soaked up with the three separate imaging sessions. The process was over just as soon as it begun and before I knew it, I was back in the dressing cubicle to swap the gown with my normal clothes.

I saw my body in the mirror again and looked a little closer this time, trying to imagine my bones beneath my skin. If my bones were deteriorating, I would have known, right? There were no signs of anything being wrong and I assumed that nothing could ever happen. After pulling my shirt down over my head, I grabbed my bag and headed out the door to go home.

Before I passed through the exit, the receptionist called out, "We'll have the results in about a week!"

I smiled and nodded and kept walking to my car.

The next week, I received a phone call from my doctor, urging me to visit her once more. She had received the results of my tests and wanted to share them with me.

"It's better if you see me in person.," she said. Thoughts started popping up in my head. I questioned why she would not just tell me over the phone, but I calmed myself by reasoning the situation in my mind. Maybe she wanted to see every one in person, I did not know. Since she had an open time slot later in the day, I decided to get it over with and go see her that afternoon.

I arrived at the office just a few hours later and I did not have to wait as long as I had before. I was her last appointment before the office closed so there was no one else in the waiting room with me. It was eerily silent but refreshingly relaxing.

"Erin, hi. Come on back."

My doctor came to get me, a rather unusual circumstance. I was used to the nurses getting me first, but I assumed she was doing it all since it was not an exam, she only had to give me some news. I sat down on the table and set my bag in my lap as she rolled her stool closer toward me and sat.

"I received your test results back earlier today, as I told you already, and I wanted to talk to you in person. Your blood test doesn't show anything too concerning, but your electrolytes are a little off. This probably had to do with you being dehydrated, but it should be something to keep in the back of your mind. Now, your bone density scans...."

She pulled out a print out from the office building I had been to the week before. On the paper were a graph, some numbers, and three pictures of my x-rays.

"Can you read that word for me?" Her finger pointed to the highlighted word on the page.

"Osteo..penia?" I had never heard of the word and I was not even sure if I was pronouncing it correctly.

"Yes, osteopenia. Do you know what that is?"

A confused look splashed across my face as I shook my head from right to left.

"I'm sure you've heard of osteoporosis, right? Well, osteopenia is like osteoporosis, just not as bad. But worse than normal bones. See, these are your scores right here. Yours are all around -1.3 when most 19 year old's are well above that. Your bones have deteriorated a fair amount, but the good news is that your bones are still growing and you can still add calcium before it's too late."

My eyes stared at the paper as I tried to take everything in. I understood what she was telling me, but how could it have happened to me? I had never been sick and I had always been healthy. My food intake could not have caused my bones to lose that much calcium in such a short period of time.

"I am going to suggest that you start talking calcium supplements every day now. There are a few brands to choose from, even generic ones that work just as fine. You don't need a prescription, it's over the counter. Got it?"

"Sure." Only, I was not sure. There had to be some mistake. Were those papers really mine? Or was I really harming my body? I always thought that I was invincible. In a split second, I realized that maybe I was not superhuman, after all.

5

POINT OF NO RETURN

I've been thinking a lot about emotions and feelings and anything related to that. Maybe I'm just going through a rough patch, hopefully that's all. It seems as though I've been feeling really down, especially at night. I hate the feeling of loneliness and emptiness. I feel like there's nothing I can do to change it. I feel like the whole world is passing me by and I'm just stuck in one place, and that I'll always be stuck in this place. I have experienced nothing and there are kids my age or younger who have been around the world, who have experienced things, who are in love, who have good friends to be with. I'm stuck here with no place to go, nothing to do, and no one to be with. I can't open up to anyone.

I'm starting to think I've become this emotionless person. I just realized that I haven't cried in the longest time, probably since camp when I freaked out over dinner. I've learned to bottle up my feelings so well when I'm with other people that I can't even let them out when I'm by myself. Crying would make me feel better, yet I can't. I have so much to say but it doesn't want to come out.

Randy, the certified EMT from camp, somehow found out that I had been sick and he wanted to know what was going on with me. We were all given a contact list with every one of our co-workers on it, in case we needed to contact them, or if we just wanted to keep in touch. Before I quit my job at camp, Randy and I had a sort of flirtatious relationship but nothing ever came out of it. He was 20 and going to a local college not far from my house; he stayed there during the summer and then was hired at camp. The other guys that I worked with seemed to be slightly immature for their age, but Randy was not. His maturity surpassed all of the other guys' and he was a gentleman, always holding doors for the girls and helping wherever there needed to be an extra hand. He seemed too good to be true on the outside.

He looked me up on the contact sheet and called my

number not too long after I got the results of my bone density scan. It was nice to hear from him, yet a bit awkward at the same time, only because we had not talked in a while.

"What are you doing Saturday night? My roommate will be out so I will have the dorm to myself, I thought it'd be nice to catch up. Especially since you left so suddenly!"

I felt guilty leaving him without giving an explanation. "I'm sorry, it's a long story. Kinda difficult. But yeah, it'd be good to hang out. I can bring over a movie, if you want."

His voice heightened with excitement. "Yeah! Bring whatever movie you want, I'm not picky."

We continued talking for about a half hour until he had to leave for class. After I hung up the phone, I realized that my "date" with Randy would be my first social outing in a long time. I was still isolating and never initiated any plans with friends on my own. Most of my friends had forgotten about me or became frustrated with my escalating craziness. I was pleased that I would be able to have some human contact for a change, with someone my own age. And with someone who I slightly had a crush on.

Saturday came around and I was all set to see Randy. I still was not sure about which movie to bring with me, but I figured that I could bring a few and we could decide together which one to watch. I dressed up in a cute top with black skinny jeans and flats, still casual but a bit more on the dressy side of what I normally wore. My hair was usually always worn down, but I decided to pull it back to keep it out of my face.

My nerves started setting in even before I left my

house, and I still had to drive across town to the college. I was not nervous about seeing him, but because I was stepping out of my comfort zone just by being social. I expected and knew that I would have a good night. Before I left, I tried to calm myself down by meditating, only it worsened my thoughts because I had no distractions. My anxieties were all I could think about.

On the 30 minute drive to Randy's college, my mind played out scenarios and I tried to pick which one I would want to happen the most. I was not sure whether to hug Randy or just say "Hey" when we met. I was not sure if it was a date or just a catch-up between friends. I was making myself anxious by creating the various outcomes in my own head. In reality, I knew I could not predict what was going to happen. I just had to take things as they came.

As I arrived at the lush college campus, I felt a bit envious of the students who were lucky enough to attend school. I was taking a break from school in order to find out what I was passionate about. I did not have a clear enough idea after my freshman year at a community college, and I liked to say that I was a sophomore. Technically, I was. I was jealous that people my age were able to live in dorms without their parents around and telling them what to do every day. I wanted to have that same responsibility, yet I was stuck at home.

Randy's dorm was not too far from where I parked, and I was very thankful because I was also worried about getting lost on the big campus. His building was secured so I had to call him on my cell phone in order to get in.

"Hey! Can you let me in?"

"What's the password??" he laughed. "Just kidding, I'll be right down."

A few seconds later, he traveled down a few flights of stairs and unlocked the door for me.

"Hey, I'm glad you could make it." He smiled as he opened the entrance.

"Me too." I was glad I could make it, even though I was still nervous.

He first showed me the lobby on the main floor. It was equip with a few flat screen televisions and some couches, along with a quaint and cozy study area. I was not sure how one was supposed to study while televisions were blasting in the background, but I liked the set-up and decorations. He led me into the elevator and pressed his floor's button. We did not say a word to each other as the elevator climbed the floors. He led me to his room, opening the door for me again.

"You have a pretty nice room here!" I looked around and saw what looked to be a four-star hotel. Every piece of furniture matched and all of the latest technological gadgets were spread throughout the small space. I had never seen a dorm room like his; I was expecting the average miss-matched, dirty college boy look.

"Yeah, my parents did all of this for me. I wasn't expecting it."

Oh, I got it. His parents must have been rich. I wondered how rich, even though that was probably rude of me to think. I also wondered if Randy was a typical "Mama's Boy." Maybe that was why he was so nice.

"Did you bring any movies? I have some here, but

we can watch whatever you want."

I pulled out a few DVDs that I stuck in my bag a few hours earlier. I shuffled through them and held up the ones that I thought he might find interesting.

"Ok. Halloween? Sin City? Spiderman? I brought 'guy' movies."

We both chuckled and he shrugged. "Pick whichever one you want to watch."

I settled on "Halloween" and handed it to him.

"Do you want a drink? I have a few beers in the fridge." He walked toward his mini stainless steel fridge, much fancier than most of the mini fridges I had ever seen.

"Ehh...sure." I was not much of a drinker. I was not of legal age to be drinking, any way, but I had had alcohol before and I knew I could handle one or a few drinks.

After he pulled the bottles out of the fridge, we sat down on the large futon placed against the wall, facing the giant flat screen television. Randy inserted the DVD into the player and the movie started to play. As I began to relax, I realized that I was more comfortable than I had anticipated. None of the problems and thoughts that I had earlier were coming into fruition. This proved that I tended to scare myself without legitimate reasons; a good lesson, I thought.

After a good hour into the movie and a few beers later between the both of us, we were very much comfortable together. I had not slept well the night before and I asked Randy if I could rest my head on his shoulder while we watched the movie. My eyelids grew heavier and heavier and we somehow managed to inch our way closer and closer to each other. By the time the movie ended, we were just short of laying down completely on the futon.

"Classic movie, never gets old." Randy said, as he turned off the television and DVD player. "Now what?"

I did not know. I only planned to watch a movie. "I don't know." At least I was being honest. "What is there to do? We can watch another movie or see what's on TV."

He looked as though he thought hard about what to do next, but he did not say a word. Instead, a leaned down to kiss me. His action startled me and left me in a bit of a shock. I was not expecting him to kiss me. I backtracked to think if I had led him on in any way. I did have a little crush on him, but I doubted it was obvious to him and I never said anything.

He smiled and leaned down again, giving me another kiss, this time longer than the first. I was starting to worry a little bit only because we had not known each other very well and I was not one to be very intimate that soon. I was confused as to how to act in the situation.

"You like that?"

What could I say? The kiss was nice, but was he asking for more? I did not know how to answer the question. I stared blankly into his eyes as he moved his way on top of me. At that point, I knew where he was heading.

"Umm..." I tried to pull away from him. "I think I should go. I just remembered I have to get something done for tomorrow."

His eyebrow raised in question. "You do? Nah, you can stay here a little longer, it's ok. You don't need to leave."

I was increasingly getting more panicked by his responses. I was not sure if the alcohol was playing into his speech or not.   "No, I'm going to go...." My voice trailed off as he placed his mouth over mine once again. His hand started roaming down my body, making me very uncomfortable and uneasy of the situation he was placing me in.

My thoughts raced as I asked myself what I should do. I was never in a similar situation before, I never had to try to get away from a guy. I knew he was stronger than I was and I already told him that I wanted to leave. What else could I do?

"You smell nice." He tried to compliment me in order for me to comply with him but his plan was not working. His grip on me was getting tighter and tighter, while my fists clenched together, waiting for everything to be finished.

His fingers tickled my skin. I could smell the beer on his breath. I stared at the ceiling and then at the clock hanging on the wall, watching the hands travel around the face as time passed.

I knew that I needed to leave before things got any worse.

"I *really* need to go." I lifted myself up from underneath his body and started standing up, only he was not happy with that decision. He pulled me back down onto the futon with so much force that my body bounced back up on the mattress.

"No. I want you to stay here." The look in his eyes was not the same look that I had seen before in him. His eyes were glossed over with some other emotion, a horrible, terrifying emotion that I did not know existed in him. I saw him before as a perfect young gentleman with manners and respect. What I saw in that moment was the exact opposite. He was not a gentleman and he was not treating me with respect. He was treating me as his object, an object he was not going to let go of until he was satisfied. A sinister grin appeared on his face, almost as if he was in a trance and not himself at all.

Tears started to well up in my eyes as my fear heightened, my fists still clenched and unable to move. He noticed the tears forming and kissed my forehead.

"Don't be scared. There's nothing to worry about."

I glanced over at the clock again to see how much time had passed. The seconds felt like minutes and time felt as if it was standing still. Everything moved in slow motion and I started to see myself as an outside observer. I was no longer a part of my body, but merely a girl watching a show. Whatever the boy was doing to the girl, I was not a part of.

I sat back and painfully watched him take advantage as she trembled and silently cried for help. There was nothing she could do. Her voice was the only thing to save her and her voice was not being heard. He seemed to enjoy her pain and failed to notice any tears that dripped down her cheeks. He was not interested in her feelings, only how he was feeling in that moment. He did not care what he was doing, and in a twisted way, he did not know he was being harmful. She continued to stare blankly, frozen with fear. She knew then that it was not his first time hurting someone else. It was too easy for him to take away a part of some one.

As if he was hypnotized, he stopped just as suddenly as he started, and moved himself to the corner of the couch so I could get up. I fixed myself, sopping up the tears with a nearby tissue, and quickly got myself out of his dorm room.

I did not have any memory of myself and the journey I made from his room to my car, but I made it there safely. And somehow, I made it home. I was safe.

6

SILENT SUFFERING

I decided last night that today would be my binge day, just because I wanted to give my body a break after depriving it for so long. Well, I took the whole binging thing to heart and ate eight donuts in ten minutes. That's a disgusting amount of food - a whole fucking box of donuts!! I don't even know why I ate that much, I've never eaten that much before in my life, I wasn't THAT hungry. It was just a goal, I guess. I set my mind to do it, and I did it, just like when I didn't eat for two days. I have no idea why I do some of the things I do. So, after that I felt disgusting, obviously, so I tried to purge t all. I tried for a good while but nothing came up. I was freaking out, "I need to get this out of me...get t out....get t out....*gag*...*spt*....ugh..." There's nothing like staring down at the toilet water with your toothbrush shoved down your throat and being disappointed in NOT being able to throw up. It's pretty twisted, isn't t? I eventually calmed myself down by stepping on the scale. It was the same as this morning so I didn't feel too bad. But I'm not eating any more donuts for a looong time.

I decided not to tell any one about what happened between Randy and me. I felt embarrassed, ashamed, guilty. I should have been able to protect myself better, I should have been more forceful, I should have screamed and yelled and punched him to get away. But I did not and it happened. It seemed like a dream, or more appropriately, a nightmare, but I knew it was real life. Since I separated myself from my body, I kept trying to convince myself that nothing ever happened. But it did. And I needed to live with that for the rest of my life.

Loneliness and depression had been dragging me down. I did not want to eat. I only wanted to sleep, sleep, sleep, and hide away from everything, hide away from the world, hide away from myself. My body was stuck in the fetal position as I drowned in the heavy blankets above me. My life seemed like it was going nowhere and I had no motivation to do anything. I laid in my bed for the majority of my days, staring at the ceiling and contemplating what I could do to end it all.

Fleeting images of horrible suffering danced through my head. I imagined how I could get away with leaving the world with hurting as few people as possible. Driving myself into a wall was not guaranteed, nor was slicing my wrists open with a razor. I thought about the failure and letting everyone down, and possibly needing to explain myself later. I would not know what to say.

I was not brave enough to end my life. I was only brave enough to get even more lost in my obsession of food, weight, and calories. I decided that I would lose even more weight. The pretend world made up in my head was my escape and I wanted to get even more lost in that world so I could not face the real world. The pretend world gave me an excuse to check out of life and to completely ignore the problems before me.

My food intake became even more limited than it had been before. I was determined to hurt myself by depriving myself. A normal, healthy intake for a 19-year-old girl was about 2,000 calories. I was eating only a third of what I should have been eating on most days, if that. I started keeping a food log of everything I was eating, just in case I forgot, even though I was able to remember my caloric intake for days on end. Calorie counts were seared into my brain and I could easily rattle off the number of calories in a given meal at any time, on any day. My brain became a huge lock box of nothing but numbers and facts used to hurt my body.

Hobbies that I had enjoyed before my obsession were not in my life any more. I used to play the guitar every day and since I started controlling my food, I had no desire to even pull the guitar out of its case. I used to enjoy reading for pleasure, yet it was too much work to even pick out a book and flip to the first page. My world was being entirely consumed by this great force. And although I had started the force on my own, it soon became its own power and started controlling me. Instead of me making my own decisions, I felt as though there was another force making the decisions for me. I was losing my ability to decide for myself and I was becoming a puppet of my own creation.

My strings were being pulled by the obsession I started. Had I known the intensity and the power of it all, I might have chosen to take a different route. But by then, it was too late and I could not turn back. I was stuck in my ever-increasing world of suffering, where pain was normal and happiness was non-existent.

I was trapped but my parents did not catch on to what was changing within me. Since I was isolated before, it seemed the same since nothing had changed from their point of view. What changed was inside my head where only I could see. What little I knew was confusing and a mix of multiple emotions, tangled together. Anger, fear, guilt, were all smashed inside of me somewhere, prying to get out in some way. I had always been taught to deal with my negative emotions myself and to not bring them up to anyone else, so it was what I did. I hid them even from myself and had no training on how to deal with the negativity.

Growing up, I thought that I was required to be

happy all of the time. I would smile and laugh, even if I was not happy or amused. My thoughts stayed inside my brain and never dared to leak out in any way. Eventually, those negative emotions had to come out in some form or another.

The way I see it, it was like a soda bottle being shaken. It was fine at first, but the more it was rattled around, the more pressure there was, and the more likely it was to explode. I had come to my exploding point, yet I chose to deal with it in an unhealthy manner.

Since my days consisted of sleeping and moping around the house, it was as if my parents had adopted a zombie for a daughter and sent me off to a far away land. My eyes were soulless and no emotion was emitted from my voice when I spoke. Going through the motions of life was not too hard, but it was not living. Going through the motions was merely existing. I was only existing and had become a shell of my former self before everything started. Instead of occupying my mind with fun activities, I chose to instead think about food.

As I watched commercials on television for fast food restaurants, I would repeatedly tell myself that that food was never going to touch my lips. That food was not fit for my consumption. Except, one day, that voice inside stayed quiet for just enough time for me to be "human" again, and so I went and bought a meal from a local fast food chain. I enjoyed the meal in my bedroom, savoring the flavor, my body thanking me for giving it some fat. And then the voice and the power took over again. I stopped myself from eating that very second and spit on the remaining food so I would not be able to eat any more. The voice told me that I was disgusting and that I was going to gain weight from just those few bites.

I looked down at the french fries and chicken and could not believe what I saw. I just willingly spat on my food. No normal person would ever do that for the same reason I did. I was terrified that the calories and fat instantly attached to my body as I ate the food. As soon as I chewed the substance, I was sure that the fat was already being shoved beneath my skin. I could feel myself growing bigger with every chew I made.

I was no longer myself, but completely a robot controlled by the monster. I never expected my curiosity to escalate so far, making me think that I was losing my sanity. I thought that by omitting certain things from my diet, it would in turn make me happy. The weight would come off, I would be more confident in myself, and my self-esteem would rise, giving me the strength that I never had before. Instead of my plan working out like I had imagined, it completely backfired and was doing the exact opposite of what I wanted.

Every time I stepped on the scale, my weight had decreased. My goal was to lose 10 pounds, until I hit that goal. My goal kept getting lower and lower and no number ever satisfied me. Once I cut out food to where I was only eating about 700 calories, barely enough to survive, I began thinking that those 700 calories were even too much. As far as I went, nothing was ever good enough, and I wanted to keep pushing myself further and further. Only I was not sure if I was physically able to keep pushing myself.

Picking out something to eat was always a difficult

task. Sometimes I would stand in front of the kitchen cabinet and blankly stare at the food for what seemed like hours. I did not have the courage to take any food off of the shelf, or I was too busy playing a scenario in my head where I was eating the forbidden food I was staring down. The voice in my head went back and forth in every decision I made, exhausting me mentally by the time I did make up my mind. A lot of the time, I walked away before the verdict was made just so I would not have to listen to fighting going back and forth between the monster and me. I knew what was right and he thought he knew what was right. He won most of the time.

By the time I lost enough weight that my pants were sliding down my body because they were too big, my body was not happy with the decisions and intense pressure I had put it under. I began having heart palpitations as a result of not treating myself well. My heart fluttered and it felt as though it was jumping out of my chest. I was worried about having a heart attack, which I knew was not an uncommon result of placing the body under so much stress. My invincibility was wearing away and for the first time, I felt human. I felt like maybe I could be hurt and that my actions may possibly do some damage.

The road I was traveling was not the road that I had planned for myself. I began to question my decisions and past actions. I thought that maybe something would need to be changed, only I felt so powerless and weak against the monster inside. It held me tight and was not going to let go anytime soon. I was afraid to fight back but I was also afraid to stand still and let it continue to rule me. I only knew that I could not fight alone. But I also knew that I was terrified to change, terrified to move at all without the advice that was being given to me 24 hours a day by the voice.

One of my darkest moments was staring into the toilet with my toothbrush hanging from my mouth, and being so depressed that I could not purge from my system the disgusting amount of food that I had just eaten. I sat alone on the bathroom floor and cried over my disappointment. I was so terribly alone, despite the voice screaming in my head. No one had any idea about what I was doing to myself or how much I was suffering.

I realized in that moment that maybe something needed to change. I knew that it was not normal for a girl of 19 to be saddened by not vomiting up the calories. Most people usually hate it when they are sick, yet I was trying to make myself sick. I stared into the water and it took me a minute to recognize the face that was staring back at me. I did not look like myself any more. My eyes were sunken and my skin was dry and more pale than usual. The look on my face was of sadness, not of happiness that I had hoped for those months ago when I started my journey. I had never seen myself in that way before and I was shocked. I could not believe that I had not seen it earlier. I was virtually a completely different person. My body was much thinner, my expressions were much more subdued, and my mind was taken over by the monster in my head. I was not myself at all. And as much as I was uncomfortable with myself in my own skin, I did not like the new person I was becoming, either.

I knew that what I was doing to myself was not

going to make me happy, but I still tried to convince myself that maybe it was not making me happy yet, but if I waited, it would eventually happen. The weight lost did not matter, only the weight that I still needed to lose. My world had become a world of numbers and distorted images. What I saw in the mirror was not what was in reality. What I thought was making me stronger was only making me weaker. I had stepped through to a land where no one could ever understand, except those who had experienced it themselves. My life was deteriorating before my eyes and there was nothing to live for any longer. My body was shutting down, begging for me to stop the torture. Everything had become so intense and I regretted my decision to ever begin the descent into hell. I was in my living hell.

In order to change things, the first thing I needed to do was to confide in someone about my troubles, no matter how hard it was going to be for me to get the words out. I was never good at speaking my mind and I usually hid what I was feeling. The fear inside of me was so overwhelming that I considered not going through with telling, but I finally pulled out the strength from within me to tell my mom.

7

FACING REALITY

I did not eat at all before I left to go out this morning. I didn't eat when my stomach was rumbling while I was reading. I didn't eat until 2:00 when I couldn't stand it anymore. Actually, I could have, but my mom was home and I wanted her to see I was eating. I had two scrambled eggs. It tasted gross, no taste at all, but I ate it. So I took a nap right before dinner, and I'm happy I did because I wasn't awake enough to think "I can't eat." During dinner, ate the corn kernel by kernel and picked at the ham. I ate, like, seven btes of ham steak and a few fork fulls of corn. I'm not very happy wth my lack of food today. I keep telling myself "Erin, just eat! Just go get something and put t in your fucking mouth! Chew and swallow!! EAT IT!" But something is always holding me back, like a part of me enjoys the hunger pains. I wish I could just eat and not have to think about t. I'm terrified of things getting worse, I don't want t to get to the point where I need to be hosptalized, yet I'm scared of things getting better, too. Getting better means eating twice the amount I have been eating. One minute I think "Ok, I just gotta eat. I can do t." and the next minute I think "What if this never goes away?" Sometimes I think nothing's wrong, and I even question whether or not I have a problem, but then I go to eat something and there's a force that just holds me back. I don't know what t is. I've never even gone on any diets before, even though I've never really been happy wth my weight, but to be like this is insane. I don't understand t. It actually feels like I'm going crazy, honestly, t's so weird.

Even though I found the strength within myself, it took weeks to gain enough courage to take the plunge and let my mom in on the secret I was hiding. The fear of the monster became overwhelming and I was unable to keep my secrets any longer. I kept my secrets for long enough and it was time to break free. I had never expressed anything so important to her before in my life and I predicted that it would be a very difficult process. Instead of physically telling her, I decided to write a note. With a note, I could pour my thoughts onto the sheet of paper and not worry about missing information. I could not be interrupted and I would not forget anything that I needed to tell.

Mom,

     I don't know if you have noticed, but I've been very isolated and have stayed in my room a lot in the past couple of months. You've noticed that I have lost weight, and I have, but I have probably lost more than you think. You and dad don't notice when I don't finish my dinners because I've been good at hiding things and lying about my actions. Mom, I think I need help. I feel like I'm going crazy. I can't let myself eat. I planned to do this, to lose weight, but t has gotten out of control. It feels like there's a monster inside of me telling me what to do. Its voice makes my decisions and I'm really not myself any more. I don't know what to do. I don't look like those girls you see on TV, the ones that are dying, so you probably don't believe me. Do you? But I needed to write this to you. I didn't want to tell you because you'd probably laugh or say t's not true. And this isn't for attention, either. I think something is wrong.

   ♥ Erin

    The night after I wrote the letter, I joined my mom while she was sitting in the living room watching television. When a commercial break came up on the screen, I walked over to her and handed her the note. My head bowed down and I shuffled back to my seat, the tears already starting to form in my eyes. She opened the letter and read silently. I held my breath as her eyes scanned the page.

As she was finished reading, she looked up at me with a nondescript expression on her face. I did not know what she was thinking and it took her a moment to speak.

"I don't know what to say to this." She skimmed the letter once more. "Are you sure? You mean, you think you have an eating disorder? How...wh...I don't get it."

The tears started to drip down my face, despite my efforts to hold them back, and I did not know what to say to her in response. I was afraid of her not believing me, and it sounded like she did not.

"Yeah, I think so. I don't know, I just need help."

Her eyes caught mine and she finally saw some of the pain, yet was so caught off-guard she had no idea what to say, either.

"Well, ok...."

I continued to cry and she stopped talking, focusing back on the television. I was not sure if she was concerned or not. I was not sure if I had just made a stupidly bad decision, or a decision that was in my best interest. I still did not know if she believed me or if she was pacifying me in the moment. I was confused at her reaction.

My tears slowed and I began to wonder if telling her was the best decision. Maybe I was supposed to keep quiet.

Days passed without any communication between us about the subject. I avoided the topic on purpose and she failed to bring it up. I sensed that she was still taking everything in and did not know how to talk about it. After three days of the situation not changing, I cautiously reminded my mom of the note.

"What do you think I should do, mom?"

"Do? About what?"

"Umm. Well...about what I wrote to you. How I think I need help or something." My voice shook a little as my nervousness increased.

"Erin, I don't know what to tell you. I don't know a lot about that kind of stuff. And you hid everything well so it's all been a shock to me. Maybe you could do some research and see what you find."

I was not thrilled with her answer. I wanted the stereotypical television mother-daughter sympathy reaction. She was supposed to tell me that she would fix everything and that it would all turn out okay. But then I realized that I was an adult, technically, and it was my problem. It was my job to fix myself and I needed to help myself.

Responsibility had always scared me. I never liked holding the responsibility for different projects because I was always afraid that I would fail. Failure was never an option for me. Now it was my responsibility to take care of myself and I was still afraid that I would fail.

After our brief conversation, I logged onto the internet in hopes to find some information about treatment centers, eating disorder facts, anything that could help me in my journey. Not too long after I started searching, I found a place not very far from my house that treated those with eating disorders. Many other centers were located throughout the country, although, I felt that it was best for me to stay close to home. After reading about the facility and its options, I came across reviews online at a different web site, where previous patients wrote about their experiences. There were a few negative reviews but the majority were positive. Reading their words made me feel not so alone, and it showed me that maybe I made the right decision to step in the direction of getting myself out of the mess.

I first thought about how others would react if I mentioned that I needed to go see a psychiatrist. There was so much taboo around the subject and I knew that others usually poked fun at just the thought. Going to see a psychiatrist meant that you were crazy, an outcast from everyone else in the real world.

Maybe I was crazy. I was in my own little world full of destruction and pain and I did not want to step into the real world. But I was not the kind of crazy that was shown in movies, the kind that were so mentally ill that they needed to be locked up and sedated on medication. I knew that the majority of those with mental illnesses looked and seemed perfectly normal, only I was afraid to be compared to the insane, unstable basket cases.

I wrote down the phone number to the center and grabbed my cell phone out of my bag. My fingers quivered as I dialed the numbers. In an automatic nervous response, I hung up the phone and took a deep breath to calm myself. It was a huge step for me to make, to start making the changes in myself in order to take a different path. I dialed the numbers again, that time staying on the line until someone picked up on the other end.

"Hello, Stafford Center for Eating Disorders, may I help you?"

8

BEGINNING OF
THE END

I have no idea what to expect. I fear that I won't be seen as sick enough for help. I'm terrified of this whole process. "If only I were skinnier. Everything will be so much better!" Well, I'm skinnier, and nothing has changed. Actually, things are worse because I can never indulge in foods I used to love. Or if I do, I feel so guilty about t and only make up for t by restricting even more the next day.

I know I'll never reach my perfect weight, because I'll just want to keep losing more and more. I thought I'd stop when I lost 10 pounds but then I wanted to lose more. I just kept on going. It doesn't stop. It will never stop without help. It's gonna be very difficult to give up this crutch of horrible eating habits. It's a horrible way of living and I need to get out before things get any worse.

But what am I supposed to do without it?

The appointment had been made with the Stafford Center for Eating Disorders and I had no idea what to expect. I was not sure if I would be taken seriously; that was probably my greatest fear. Since I did not look like the stereotypical girl with an eating disorder that everyone saw in the media, I was afraid that I did have to look like that in order to warrant professional help. Even though I knew I was going to see professionals about my problem, I still worried that the stereotype was real even in doctors' eyes. I kept picturing the doctor laughing in my face after telling him that I think I needed help, and in response, he would say, "Why are you here??" The monster was trying to trick me and it seemed to be working. Was I really sick enough to need help? I felt like death a lot of the time, but I was sure that there were others who needed more help. Would I be wasting the doctor's time? I tried to rationalize my habits in order to try to skip out on the appointment, but eventually, I knew I had to go through with it.

On the day before my scheduled time, I drove by the hospital where the center was located. I did not want to get lost on my way and be late to see the doctor so I made a test run. It was not hard to get to the center, but as my car drove by and I looked at the building, I felt my heart beat harder. It was the place where I would be coming for help. Was I really ready for it? I imagined what it looked like on the inside and tried to picture the different patients locked in on the other side of the door. I wondered if any of them looked like me, thought like me, was alone like me.

That night, I could not get myself to fall asleep. Thoughts kept popping into my head and my anxiety rose with every ridiculous fake situation I imagined. In order to calm myself and focus on something other than my intrusive thoughts, I turned on the television and hoped that the background noise of people talking would put me to sleep. It did not work. I tossed and turned in my bed for hours, going back and forth on my decision to drive back to the center in the morning. There was a 24-hour notice cancellation policy, but I wondered if I could cancel if I came up with a good excuse. The problem was I had no excuse. I was going to have to bite the bullet and go. With four hours of hopeful peaceful rest ahead, I finally closed my eyes and drifted off into dreamland.

When I awoke the next morning, I forgot for a minute that the appointment. Until my mom came in soon after my eyes opened to the morning light and reminded me. If I had to go, I didn't want to roll out of bed a few minutes before and look like a slob, so I sat up, wiped my eyes, and got out of bed with enough time to take a shower, properly get ready, and try to relax.

My mom came with me to the center for moral

support, as she did not need to be with me since I was over the age of 18. I was legally an adult. I did not want to be by myself in a strange place. She also offered to drive which gave me a chance to calm myself down and prepare for what was about to happen. When we arrived, my mom turned off the car and looked at me.

"This is a good thing. I'm glad you're doing this for yourself." She seemed genuinely satisfied with my decision, despite her overwhelming confusion through the whole process.

"Thanks." I half-smiled and gripped my hand around the door handle. "Ok. This is it."

We both exited the car and walked towards the center. It was an old, red-brown brick building that stood on a plot of carefully manicured lawns. I imagined the building as an old horror film scene, as if there were stormy skies and bats flying around the rooftop. It may as well have been from a horror film, based on my fear. My palms were sweaty and I could hear my pulse thumping in my ears. Once I took that step in, there was no chance of turning around again. I was about to be led back on the path of which I tried to avoid in the first place.

The waiting room was darker than most waiting rooms I had encountered in the past. The paint on the walls was a deep, dark blue color, and the furniture was very modern for an office setting. My eyes roamed around the room and I spotted a few other girls sitting, waiting for their appointments. None of us made any eye contact; I just assumed it was common practice to avoid anyone at those types of places. I asked myself if they were embarrassed to be sitting there or if they really wanted to be there, because I myself had a twinge of embarrassment at the pit of my stomach.

I thought it was silly to need help for not eating. Eating was a simple human function and it was not normally a difficult thing to do. That is, until the mental part came into the picture. I did not want to be seen as crazy and I did not want anyone to know I was there.

Even though we did not make eye contact, I noticed their bodies and could not help but to compare mine to theirs. They were all skinnier. I was the fattest one in the room. At least, that was the truth in my head. Were they judging me or did they think I was fat? I walked over to sign myself in and was asked whom I was there to see.

"Dr. Hoffman. It's my first time here."

The receptionist looked down at the schedule sheet.

"Ah, yes, you must be Erin."

I nodded as she opened a drawer and started flipping through papers. She grabbed a sheet, then another, and still a few more, and placed them all on a clipboard.

"Here you go, you have to fill all of these out. Just bring them back to me when you're finished, alright?"

"Ok. Thanks." I was lucky I brought my mom with me because I was now worried that there would be questions I did not have the answers to. We sat down and I started to fill out the papers, making sure to print neatly so it was legible. As I continued to write, a few more girls walked into the waiting room and sat down. It crossed my mind that there were many patients coming to the center, which surprised me. I did not know anyone else but they seemed to be doing very good business with the amount of people walking through the doors.

After I completed all of the paperwork, all I had left to do was wait. The minutes passed by slowly and I looked at my watch multiple times to make sure time was still moving. I flipped through several magazines sitting on the coffee table next to me but the reading material did nothing to distract myself from the wait. Without noticing, a man in a dark suit appeared from the hallway.

"Erin? I'm Dr. Hoffman, nice to meet you. Come on back."

I followed him through a maze of narrow hallways leading to the back of the building. The décor matched the waiting room -- it all went very well together. He led me to his office and allowed me to choose which seat I wanted to sit in. To the right of me against the wall sat a young woman.

Dr. Hoffman directed his hand toward the stranger.

"This is Dr. Whitley, she's here observing today. Do you mind if she sits in with us?"

It was my first appointment and as if I was not nervous enough, I had an audience, too.

"No, I don't mind."

The doctor pulled out a packet of papers that were stapled together and looked up at me.

"So. Tell me why you're here."

That was a loaded question. I did not know where to begin so I started babbling about my desire to be happy and attaching that with being thin. The more I spoke, the less I made sense. I felt like I was pleading my case to a judge and I was failing miserably at it.

He seemed to understand, though, and he started asking questions from the papers he sat in front of him.

"I have a lot of questions here and it might take a while, but these are for us to get to know you better, so that we can help you in the best way possible."

The questions varied from family history to my current food intake to how I was feeling to past histories of any other deviant behavior. No doctor had ever asked me so many questions and I had never revealed so much about myself before. Now that he knew everything, I was worried that he would dismiss me from his office and tell me that I didn't need to be there, that I was just on a silly diet. I was sure that he had seen many patients in his career that were far worse off than I was, so why did I think he would have time for me? I was not in grave danger.

He glanced at the evaluation and asked me to go back to the waiting room while he reread my answers. I was sure that he sent me out so he could think of a gentle way to tell me that I was being ridiculous and that I was wasting his time by being there.

I sat down in the waiting room once again and told my mom everything that had gone on.

"I don't think I need to be here. I don't think I'm that sick, I don't want to waste anyone's time."

My mom took my hand in hers.

"You're not wasting anyone's time. If you think you need to be here, you need to be here."

But I was not completely sure whether I needed to be there. Could I kick the obsession on my own? Did I really need professional help? Many people were able to get rid of bad habits so why was I not strong enough to pull myself out of the trenches? I was not strong enough for anything. Just as I completed my thought, Dr. Hoffman strutted down the hall again, his tie swaying back and forth with the motion of his stride.

"Come on back again, Erin."

I once again followed him down the hallway, passing multiple closed doors and a few pieces of artwork. Once we stepped into his office, I sat in the same chair that I chose before. I did not like change. Dr. Whitley had not moved from her seat, only her position changed from the last time I saw her.

Dr. Hoffman pulled out my papers yet again in order to remember what he wrote down.

"So, I've looked over all of your notes and after consulting with a few colleagues, we think it would be best for you to go into our Intensive Outpatient Program. Would you be willing to do that?"

My eyes stared at the floor as the panic began to increase within me.

"Do you think I need it? I mean, I didn't think it was that serious, I just needed some help."

"Yes, I think you need it. No one has ever told me that they think their case is serious, no one ever feels sick enough. But I'm telling you, you do need help and it's best if you get it sooner rather than later."

"Well...what is the Intensive Outpatient Program?"

"The Intensive Outpatient Program, or IOP for short, is our program that runs from Monday through Thursday for four hours per day. You'll have dinner there and you'll have a few groups. I can have Dr. Whitley get you a copy of the information, if you'd like."

"Yeah, that'd be good." The young woman stepped out of the office and returned very soon after with a thin packet filled with information about the program. "Well...I'm not sure. You see, I don't have health insurance right now, and this would be really expensive. I'm not sure if my family can afford it." I told him the truth, although I was secretly relieved that I had a legitimate excuse.

"I'll tell you what. I'll give you a chance to improve on your own. I'll set you up with a therapist and a nutritionist, and you can see me in about a month. We'll see how you do on your own and then we can re-evaluate after. I can't force you to do the program, your parents can't force you to do the program, although, I would highly recommend it if your situation gets any worse. Alright?"

His plan was fair, although now I was going to have to see a therapist and nutritionist. I had never been to either, but I was glad that I did not have to sign into the program that day.

"Ok. I'll set up an appointment with you for a month. What about the therapist and nutritionist?"

"I'll have them call you at home, you'll hear from them soon."

Through with the meeting, I stood up from my chair and tried to escape as fast as I could without being too obvious.

"I'll see you in a month, then."

"Ok, thanks." My legs sped up as I traveled down the hall, eventually leading to my mom still sitting in the waiting room.

"I'm ok for now. I need to make an appointment, though. I'll tell you everything in the car."

9

THERAPY FOR
MY MIND

A few days later, I received a call from the Stafford Center for Eating Disorders. On the other end was a woman calling to make the appointments for me to see a therapist and nutritionist. She told me that I would be seeing Dr. Pitts and that there was currently a waiting list to see a nutritionist so I would have to make an appointment at a later date. I agreed to see Dr. Pitts the following Tuesday afternoon.

I did not know what to expect. The images of therapists I had seen on television and in the movies had skewed my opinion of them. From taking in stereotypical traits from the media, I pictured that most therapists were older men with a horrible fashion sense, wearing high-water pants and bow ties. They all wore glasses and clashed their patterns together, making them look as if they dressed themselves in the dark with no mirror. I imagined that therapy sessions were spent with the patient lying on a long couch as the doctor listened to him with a giant writing pad. Sometimes, the patient would be recorded for future reference.

Going to therapy had been sort of a taboo subject with most people. I had learned that many people do go to therapy, but that few were willing to openly talk about it. Were they not supposed to be learning how to be more open in therapy? Now that I would be going to therapy, I did not want to let anyone know. I did not want my other family members to whisper about me, and I planned to lie to friends if I was asked about where I needed to be or where I had been.

So with all of these preconceived thoughts already in my head, it was hard to start therapy with a non-judgmental outlook.

The following Tuesday appeared in no time and I drove back to the center, to the same building where I met Dr. Hoffman. I waited in the same room and signed in with the same receptionist, only I did not need to fill out the stack of paperwork again. On the table sat a recent copy of "People" magazine so I chose to skim through the pages to waste some time. Before I reached anything interesting, I heard my name.

A tall, older man with glasses, khaki pants, and a

bow tie walked toward me. He absolutely looked like the stereotypical therapist I had seen on television and pictured in my mind. I could not believe my eyes and I silently laughed to myself.

"I'm Dr. Pitts, how are you today?" He reached out to shake my hand and I complied with a weak half-shake.

"Ok." I responded. I always answered 'Okay.'

He led me through the same hallway I walked the week earlier. I passed by Dr. Hoffman's closed office door and continued to Dr. Pitts' office a few doors down. His office was not as big but it had a similar decor and view. There was only one window in the room and it faced the busy road next to the building.

In the room sat four chairs; one was obviously the chair paired with the desk, one was an extra seat along the wall, and the other two were faced toward each other. I was not sure which chair was his -- did it matter? I did not want to make the mistake of taking his chair so I sat in the seat further away from the desk chair. He sat down across from me and my first therapy session officially began.

In order for Dr. Pitts to get to know me better, he held in his hand a sheet of questions, much like the questions asked by Dr. Hoffman. I wondered why he did not just look over the other evaluation but I did not ask him why. I was not sure whether I was allowed to speak up and ask questions or whether I was only to answer and follow the doctor's lead.

Besides his appearance, therapy was nothing like I had imagined. There was no long couch for me to lie on and the office was much smaller than the fancy office suites on television. After he was finished with the questions he had prepared, he asked me simply, "Why are you here?"

Why was I there? Did he not look over Dr. Hoffman's notes? Was that a rhetorical question or did he legitimately want me to answer him? I stared at the beige carpet in front of my feet until I could think of a decent answer.

"Umm..." I scratched my forehead and wrinkled my nose in thought. "Well...my eating habits and calorie counting has gotten pretty obsessive. I felt like I was going crazy so I thought I should get some help. So, here I am."

He looked back at me and shifted his lip to the side of his mouth.

"Hmm. Ok." His pen scrawled words on the paper and my stare met the carpet again.

Silence filled the room and I began to fidget around and play with my fingers. Silence made me nervous in new situations. It made me uncomfortable, uneasy, worried. I figured that as long as some one was talking, things were okay. But with no one talking, the silence was killing me.

After his long scribble, he asked me another question.

"Do you think you are depressed?"

For that question, I had to think quite a bit. I had only known myself to be depressed, but I was not sure if I really was depressed, or if that was just how everyone felt. The media me did a great job of putting up the illusion that everything was supposed to be happy all of the time, and I tried to buy into it. But in reality, it was not always a happy place all of the time and people were allowed to be sad. I just saw the real truth, the horror, the unfortunate events, and ignored the positive in everything. My view was always covered with a gloomy haze and when the color shined through, I fanned the haze to cover it up again. Living in the fog was sad, but safe.

I had spewed out everything to Dr. Pitts without realizing I was speaking.

"Wow. You're really fucking depressed."

I could not believe what I had just heard. Were therapists supposed to talk that way to their patients? My eyes widened in disbelief and to be sure I heard correctly, I had to ask him to repeat what he just said.

"I said, you're really fucking depressed. I figured you were but your explanation proves it in a big way."

My hands started to fidget again, my fingers rubbing up against each other to try to minimize the anxious tension building up inside of me. I did not know how to respond to his comment and I was not sure if he said it as a test, or if that was how he talked to his patients. I tapped my foot on the ground and just kept thinking, unable to speak.

He caught on to my anxious state.

"What are you thinking?"

I did not want to tell him what I was thinking. If I told him, I would have had to tell him that I thought that maybe he was the one that needed the therapy. I did not want to offend him but secretly I was holding back the urge to leave and never come back for another session.

"Nothing."

"Nothing? You have to be thinking about something. Come on."

He was deliberately trying to get some emotion out of me but I was not going to give in. I was not going to let a stranger see anything but contentment. I was fine. I tried to convince him and myself at the same time.

"I'm really not thinking about anything." I wanted him to move on to a different subject so I could focus on something else.

The session finally ended after 50 minutes of awkward silences and awkward questions. He did not get too much information out of me and I did not really care. I did not feel comfortable talking to him. I left his office in a rush without setting another appointment. From what I could see, he was the one who needed a shrink, and I was not going to trust a therapist who sent off that vibe. How was I supposed to build a relationship with someone who told me, flat our, that I was "really fucking depressed?"

Because I failed to make another appointment, Dr. Hoffman ultimately got word of it and he made a phone call to my house a few days later to hear my reason. I did not have a reason, other than I did not want to go anymore and that I was not comfortable. But the thing was, I made a deal with Dr. Hoffman when I saw him last. Since I did not want to continue on with therapy, I was obligated to go into the program he told me about. Technically, I was not forced to go since I was over the age of 18 and legally an adult. But I knew that it would be in my best interest if I did go through with it, no matter how much I did not want to.

Two weeks later, I was back in the office where I made my therapy escape. Dr. Hoffman set up and appointment for me to be evaluated, yet again. Even though I knew that I was being asked important questions, I was tired of answering them all and I liked giving one-word answers. During the evaluation, I was required to get my vitals checked by a nurse to see if I was medically stable enough to go to the outpatient program instead of the hospital inpatient program.

A nurse brought me back to a little secluded room to perform the tests. First, I laid down on the floor and she wrapped a blood pressure cuff around my arm. I laid there and tried to relax as the machine pumped the cuff, then stopped and slowly deflated.

"You have a very fast heart beat. Are you nervous?" The nurse asked. I liked her. She seemed to really enjoy her job and seemed genuinely happy to help patients.

"Yeah, I am, but my pulse is always high."

"Stand up for me." The cuff stayed on my arm and she pressed the button for the cycle to repeat. "Do you feel dizzy? Lightheaded?"

"Nope." It was actually unusual that I was not feeling dizzy or seeing spots. That had become the norm in my every day life and I had gotten used to it. The spots eventually went away after closing my eyes for a few seconds, after my weary body adjusted.

"Do you know what orthostatic hypotension is?"

I had never heard of it and before I could mumble a 'no,' she started her explanation.

"When your body goes from laying down to standing up, your blood pressure usually stays about the same in both positions. Yours drops significantly after you stand up. The blood rushes down to the lower part of your body and your body cannot cope as well. It could mean that you're dehydrated."

"Oh. I got sick a while ago from being dehydrated. I thought I was ok now." I fooled myself into thinking that since I did not physically feel sick all of the time, my body was doing just fine.

After the tests, I was given a bundle of paperwork and another packet of papers explaining the program.

"When you're finished filling these out, just give them back to me, and you're free to go. The program starts this afternoon."

This afternoon? I did not know that I was going that day. At first, I started to freak out because I had not prepared myself, but then I thought that it would be better to start that day. Instead of having to wait another 24 hours, at least, I only had to wait a few hours.

But those hours were so long.

There was nothing for me to do for those few hours so I decided to try and draw to pass the time. It had been a hobby I had all but given up for the eating disorder. I pulled out a Sharpie marker from my bag, along with a book sized Moleskine journal I always carried around with me. My fingers flipped to find an empty page and I began to draw. The felt tip of the marker touched the smooth surface of the paper and suddenly I felt what I had been missing from my life. When I drew, my emotions were able to seep out onto paper instead of staying scrambled, stuck in my head. The marker floated across the paper ever so easily and the time passed by quickly. I drew without thinking, with all of my attention focused on the task at hand. My mind was not focused on food or weight for once. I missed the times in my life when I could relax and ease my mind and not think about anything. Those times were very rare, as my head was always filled with images of me being thin and the food that I was or was not going to eat.

After quite a bit of time passed, I lifted up my hand and focused on the image on the page that I had just drawn. I drew without thinking too much about it and I was surprised at what I saw, the black figure sitting stark on the white page. It was en eye with a single tear dripping from its lower eyelid. It was me crying out for help. In all of the obsessions, I failed to notice the intensity of my sadness within. Focusing on the food and the drive to be better made me forget about being depressed. It gave me a way out, a way to ignore the emotion I did not want to feel. I did not know how to express sadness most of the time, and I was embarrassed to cry in front of others. My way of showing that emotion was by trying to show it physically by depriving myself. That way, others would need to ask if I was alright. Yet, even if I was asked, I still did not want to answer. I wanted to be cared for but I also did not want to show I needed the care.

I kept drawing in my book and glanced down at my watch. I only had 20 minutes until IOP started. My drawing was a clear sign of my need for help but it did not change my feelings of not wanting to let go of the crutch I had been using to escape.

10

INTENSE PATH
TO RECOVERY

I stood in front of the brick building for a few moments, staring through the glass paned door, debating on whether or not to step through that entryway. After thinking of the consequences of not entering, my courage finally allowed me to make my way through. I entered the unknown world of treatment where I had no clue as to what would go on. No one else was in the waiting room but me. I started to question if I had made it to the right place, or if I was late for the day. I could feel my heart beating faster and my feet started tapping on the floor without me thinking. The room was dark, quite unlike most medical offices I had seen in the past. It seemed like a more upscale kind of place but it was intimidating at the same time.

After a few minutes of silently sitting by myself, a few girls made their way through the front door. They were giggling and acted as if they had known each other forever. I decided that I would wait for them to say something to me first, so I continued to sit in silence.

"Did you do your homework?" one of the girls asked. She was loud and appeared to be very outgoing.

"Aww, damn. No! Crap." The girl next to her quickly fished through her notebook and found the homework that was supposed to be completed.

Homework? This place was not school, why would I need to do homework? I also was not told that I would need a notebook and pen, either. My first day was starting out not so well. As if I was not nervous enough, being with completely new people and being unprepared had me wanting to run out of the door and drive back home.

I must have started to show my fear and one of the girls across the room spoke.

"Is this your first day?"

I nodded in response. "Yeah."

"Ohh. Don't worry, you'll be fine. We were all really nervous on our first day. It gets easier." She smiled and tried to comfort me, and although I appreciated her advice, it did not make me feel much better.

"Thanks."

A door located on the other side of the waiting room opened and a head popped out to greet us all.

"Come on in!"

I guessed she was the therapist, but I was not sure. There was definitely no turning back now. I had reached the point of no return. I was terrified with surprisingly a sense of relief mixed in. Maybe treatment would be the beginning of my chance to change things around for myself. Even though I did not necessarily want to change, I knew that what I was doing was not in my best interest.

We all walked into the wide-open room and took a seat. Each seat was upholstered very nicely, probably to make patients a bit more comfortable. After all, it was therapy, not a time to have fun. The room was decorated much like the waiting room with dark colors and big picture windows looking out to the massive oak trees in the yard. Our seats were arranged in a circle, making us face each other. I was convinced that the chairs were set up that way on purpose, in order to make groups more uncomfortable for newcomers. And I was so very uncomfortable.

"Hi, guys, this is CBT. If you're new here, my name is Dr. Serrano. Can anyone explain what CBT is to the new patients?"

My brain zoned out and I could not hear the explanation of what CBT was, nor did I particularly care at that point. I was more focused on the young therapist sitting before me. She looked not much older than me and I guessed she had just recently earned her doctorate. Her overall look was very put together and she could have stood in for a model in a catalogue. Instead of paying attention to what was going on, I could only think of how the newly educated therapist could possibly know how to treat eating disorders.

There was a young, attractive doctor, I was sure very intelligent, but how could she possibly relate to us? I doubted she ever had to struggle with low self-esteem, judging on her appearance alone. I had always assumed that others who seemed put together on the outside were put together on the inside.

I never imagined that someone who looked confident could have been very self-conscious like me. In my world, anyone who was good looking, confident, and sure of themselves was immune to any negative thoughts running around in their mind. Their life was well organized, they had a great job and many friends, and they were not depressed. I pictured them to have a perfect life, a life that I desired to have.

My brain tried to focus back on to what was going on with the group. The doctor looked at me and asked if I understood what was just explained.

"Um. Could you explain it again? I'm sorry." She and everyone else around must have though I was stupid.

"Sure. CBT is short for Cognitive Behavioral Therapy. In short, this therapy is designed to dispute your thoughts and challenging them into thoughts that are more realistic. For example, say you were thinking, "My pants feel tighter so I must've gained weight." You could dispute that by thinking, "My pants feel tighter but it's because I just ate dinner, not because I gained weight." Make sense?"

I shook my head to let her know that I understood. It was not such a hard concept to grasp, although I was sure it was going to be hard to challenge thoughts that had been repeated over and over again.

Dr. Serrano pulled out a stack of papers and passed them around the room, instructing each of us to take one sheet. When I received my copy, I looked down and read the title: Self-Esteem Defined.

How ironic that I would be working on self-esteem on my first day in the program. My brain was already fired up about it, and by coincidence, I received a worksheet on the same subject. Self-esteem was a tough topic for me. I always thought that my self-esteem was pretty good, until I realized that I was only pretending. In reality, my self-esteem was never very high. My mind drifted to my three-year-old self, the little girl who thought poorly of herself and her body.

My self-esteem had always been connected to my body in some way. If I was not very good at something, I took it out on myself and automatically thought that it was because of my physical being on the outside. I remember watching television and realizing that all of the women would equate their likeability to their body size, shape, or appearance. If a man did not like a woman, she thought it was because she was ugly. Or fat. Or too tall. It was never because they did not have a connection or that they just did not get along. My brain had been wired to think that my faults always came back to my body.

Besides my physical appearance, I felt as though I was never good at anything I did, or if I was good, I was not good enough. I wanted to be perfect. I wanted to make no mistakes and for everyone to be proud of me. I wanted to be the smartest so my parents could go up to their friends and show me off. I imagined them pointing to me with cheesy grins on their faces, gloating about me and how I did so well. Sometimes they did, at least when they were putting on a show.

At home, it was a different story. My faults were always pointed out and criticized while my accomplishments were minimized. I actually was an intelligent student and I always brought home report cards filled with A's and B's -- except when it came to math. I figured that I was born without the gene that was able to process numbers and calculations. When I advanced to higher levels of math, I could not grasp the concepts like many of the other students. Instead of receiving A's and B's like in the other subjects, I received C's, and even a few D's.

On those report cards, my eyes simply focused on the math grades and failed to notice the others, even though they were very good grades and something to be proud about. My dad pointed out the fact that I was not doing very well in math, failing to even mention the other grades most of the time.

I was stupid. Dumb. A failure.

I learned to ruminate on the more negative aspects and completely ignore the positive. It hurt my self-esteem since the negative completely overruled the positive. Instead of sharing my emotions with someone, anyone, I pushed them aside for another time. Only, that time never came, and so my emotions had built up inside for years. Every negative fact I had heard about myself and my performances were clung to me. I remembered them far more clearly than anything positive mentioned.

By the time my thoughts started to wind down and

my writing was completing on the sheet, it was time to share our thoughts with the group.

"Who wants to start?"

I sat in my seat, silently staring at the floor, waiting for someone else to chime in first. I did not particularly want to talk and there was no way I was going first.

"I'll go!" The outgoing personality who spoke to me volunteered to share. I learned that her name was Danielle and her story was very similar to my own. She also never felt good enough and wanted to be perfect at everything she accomplished. I felt comfort in knowing that I was not alone in the struggle to accept myself. Although I knew I had qualities that were great for me, it was not enough, and I saw that in someone else.

By looking at her, I would not have guessed she had self-esteem problems. Just as I judged the doctor based on outside appearances, I had judged her, too, even before the exercise. She looked confident as well, yet it was all a front. I wondered how well I acted in front of other people in order to hide how I was really feeling.

I realized that everyone in group was hiding behind the fake wall of the eating disorder in order to show their fake self-esteem. None of us wanted to show our true selves for fear of rejection and judgment. We all felt so low about ourselves and had tricked everyone around us. It was a connection between us all, yet I knew it would be a great obstacle for me to overcome eventually.

11

YOU NEED MONEY
FOR THAT

After two weeks of working hard in the program, fate decided to throw in another problem for me to deal with at the same time. I received a bill in the mail for the first few days of treatment. Since I had no health insurance, my parents were going to have to pay for everything. That meant dipping into my father's retirement fund and cashing in other financial stocks in order to pay for my care. My eyes scanned through the lengthy bill and stopped when it came to the bold, black print, indicating what we owed to the hospital.

$1,000 for three days in the program. 12 hours total. 9 hours of therapy and 3 hours for dinner. I could not believe the outrageous price that had been placed on a treatment plan to help save lives.

Immediately, I felt guilty. Before I started, my parents agreed to pay the amounts due and they knew what the amounts would be. But I only had a vague idea and it was even more shocking when the days were added up and staring at me in large, bold print. I felt guilty that they were going to shell out thousands of dollars just for me, for something that I had brought on myself, any way. Thousands of dollars that could be spent on much more important things were going to be used for my selfish need and me. I did not want to take away their hard-earned money. I felt as though I was not worthy enough of that kind of price tag. I assumed that once my parents saw the numbers adding up, they would pull me out of the program, but would still keep me in long enough to get something out of it.

I was scared to show my mom the bill, so being the clear-and-outgoing-communicator I was, I left the bill in front of her chair on the kitchen table. I did not want to see a freak out reaction if I showed her myself so I avoided the situation altogether and left it for her to read alone.

I did not want to be the cause of any financial problems my parents could run into. They wisely saved their money and planned it out so they could live comfortably after retiring. Because of me, their security would now be tampered with. Their hard work would be dwindled away because of my decisions and actions. I felt selfish for knowing that they would now have to pay for me. Even though it was for something important, a legitimate medical issue, I felt that it was not important enough.

Because the medical issue was an eating disorder, my thoughts screwed around with me and convinced me that an eating disorder was not really a serious medical problem. I did not have cancer or another life threatening disease. I brought on my eating disorder, I caused it. Not only that, but I was an adult. My parents were not legally responsible for me any more but they agreed to pay for my treatment. I thought that I should have been paying my bills and not relying on my parents. I was 19 years old, not a helpless 4 year old who knew nothing about financial responsibilities. My own bank account stored money for me to pay a percentage but my parents had insisted that I needed to save my money for my future.

After being in the program for a while, I was starting to become more comfortable with the people around me and I started to open up a bit. The group knew me on the surface and also knew some underlying issues I kept inside, hidden from everyone else. I was slowly learning how to let others in on my thoughts and showing my real self, something that I had not done too often.

One group in the program was called Interpersonal Therapy and it was based on addressing all of the issues we were having within ourselves and the people around us. I felt that I needed to bring up the subject of the medical bills. I wanted to hear the group's opinion and see if they agreed with me. Even though I was getting to be more comfortable in the group setting, I still had not started a topic yet. I waited for others to speak first and if I had something to say,

I would chime in. None of my issues were the main focus and I was anxious to bring it up in the first place.

"This is IPT...." Another doctor, Dr. Reed, lead the IPT group. She was another young woman like Dr. Serrano who seemed to be very confident in herself and her abilities as a doctor. Her personality was quirky and she enjoyed making jokes. We laughed at her unique facial expressions and sense of humor, a great relief in such an intense setting.

"I heard you all were pretty talkative at dinner, so you guys should be raring to talk in here! Right??"

All of us eyed each other and smirks appeared on everyone's face. Of course, we enjoyed talking at dinner where we were able to freely talk by ourselves, even though some topics were off limits, but therapy was not as enjoyable. No one enjoyed serious talk, especially since it was what we had avoided for years and years. We were able to talk about superficial topics with no problem, yet we were not able to delve into our emotions and let people know how we were really feeling.

Because of this, IPT was sometimes awkward, especially at the beginning of every session. Our heads bowed down and our eyes never left the carpet. We all hoped that someone would talk in order to disrupt the awkward silence that filled the room. Even when there was a discussion going on, many of us were afraid to give our opinions, for fear of being judged. We were all worried about saying something wrong because we were stuck with each other every day. We did not want to hurt anyone's feelings, even if our thought was truthful and was the right advice.

The session did start with silence, but I chose to do

something I had not done before. I spoke up and volunteered to share my story first.

"Erin! What do you have for us today?"

I was not sure what I was doing, I did not know what I was going to say. I was afraid that I was wasting time. What if there was something else that another patient wanted to talk about? My issue could have been so trivial compared to their problem. So I started by saying that I felt stupid by bringing it up in the first place.

Dr. Reed began speaking immediately after I said I felt stupid.

"How can she dispute that thought?"

Almost instantly, the others began to shout out disputations for my thought.

"You're not wasting our time. It's why we're here."

"Nothing that needs to be talked about here is stupid!"

"We all feel like others are more important. It's what got us here in the first place."

They were all very right. The group as a whole was amazing at disputing thoughts, but when it came to our own thoughts, we were horrible. Somehow, we convinced ourselves that the disputations for others were not applicable to our own situations. Everyone else could receive help but us. Everyone else could be happy but us. It was difficult to apply our own advice to ourselves.

After hearing everyone's thoughts, I continued speaking, without prefacing it by saying I felt stupid. My hands started rubbing together and my foot tapped the ground. I was still hesitant to say anything.

"Well...we got the bill from the hospital today. It's for $1,000. My parents said that they would pay for treatment, since I don't have health insurance right now, but I feel really guilty for making them pay. I feel like I'm wasting their money and they shouldn't have to use their money for me, and I brought all of this on myself anyway. It's not their problem, it's mine, and I should pay for it."

The group thought for a minute. Some of them had been in similar situations and they had to talk through it, as well.

Carrie, an 18-year-old college student, sat across the room from me. She always amazed me with her unique fashion sense and her hairstyles. I was pretty sure that I had not seen her in the same outfit twice. She began to speak.

"I went through this the last time I was in treatment. I was not in school and I was dropped from my parents' health insurance. They had to pay for me and they kind of struggled, but they always reassured me that they didn't care what they had to do, that they just wanted to take care of me. I'm sure your parents think the same way. Your parents love you and just want you to get better."

I smiled and accepted her advice. My thoughts tried to dispute hers, but I tried to ignore them and focus on what she said.

To my surprise, a few others said the same thing, that my parents loved me and I should not worry about it. They mentioned that money would be lost but that I was much more important than money. I tried to accept that I ultimately was more important. Sometimes it seemed as though money was the most important thing in the world, but it was going to take a while for it to set in.

After everyone spoke and let me know what they thought about the situation, Dr. Reed asked the group a question.

"Erin doesn't think an eating disorder isn't as dangerous, say, as cancer. Can anyone explain why it is life threatening?"

We were taught the risks of eating disorders quite a few times. Anytime anyone said that their eating disorder was not serious, the discussion of how much of an impact it plays in our lives popped up. Dr. Reed wanted our brains to be seared with the information so we would never forget the dangers of eating disorders.

"Infertility."

"Loss of bone mass."

"Dehydration."

"Dry skin and hair."

"Anemia."

"Muscle wasting."

The room went silent as we all contemplated the risks involved.

"What about death?" Dr. Reed pointed out the most dangerous consequence of all, leaving us with our eyes widened with nothing to say. "Do you ever think about that? It's a possibility. Eating disorders have the highest mortality rate of any psychiatric illness. I want you all to write that down so you don't forget."

I jotted down the statement. Death was such a strong word and I never truly thought about it as a consequence before.

Eating disorders were deadly and I thought that I was safe from the risk. I felt guilty about my parents needing to pay medical bills, but it was a life-threatening illness after all. If I was diagnosed with cancer, I would not have felt as guilty, but the stigma of mental illnesses made me feel as if it was my entire fault. Ultimately, I knew that I did not choose to have an eating disorder, yet I somehow figured that it would be easy to overcome because it was all in my head. But it was not.

12

NUMBERS DO MATTER

I first entered the Intensive Outpatient Program just slightly underweight for my age and height and I knew that I would need to gain a few pounds in order to reach my goal weight. For patients who needed to gain weight, the program calculated goal weights based on height. Personally, I was not too happy with their calculation, and I knew the others were not too excited about it, either. I did not know of any patients who would willingly allow themselves to gain weight and be completely content with it. I thought that my goal weight was far too much, but I knew that it was only the eating disorder telling me that. Realistically, I had no idea how much I should have weighed. Their calculation for my goal weight was actually a healthy number for my height but my distorted thinking thought otherwise. For such a long time, my brain had been processing various numbers and trying to rationalize unhealthy low weights that I thought were all right for my body. Logically, I knew that the added weight would not kill me, but the journey to reach it was not an easy one.

We were all advised multiple times that the numbers on the scale did not matter. We were more than numbers flashing on the screen. We were people with depth and character and personalities. Numbers were not important. That is, unless weight gain was required.

Since I was expected to make the number on the scale increase every time I hopped on it, I was always torn on the results. Half of my head sided with the eating disorder and I hoped that the number would go down, giving me that rush of knowing that I had lost weight. The other half of my head sided with my recovery self and hoped that the number would budge up just a little bit, moving me closer to my goal weight, leaving less weight for me to gain.

I dreaded stepping on the hospital scale twice per week. Even though my weight was supposed to get higher, the thought of my body adding extra mass was horrifying to me. No matter what the outcome, though, the number always affected my mood.

I remember specifically one day during the program. The weather was unseasonably warm and I drove to the hospital with my car windows down and the music blaring through my speakers. I was in a great mood for no apparent reason. And then I remembered that I was to be weighed that day. My thoughts started arguing back and forth in my head as I anxiously awaited my turn to step on the scale. Sometimes, I was urged to turn my back to the scale in case I did gain weight, but I always wanted to know the exact number. The number was important. It gave me a sense of control, regardless of which way it moved. On good days, my mood would crash in a split second if that number increased. It did not matter how I was feeling before my eyes saw the outcome, it only mattered that I did, in fact, gain the weight. No matter how little, I swore that I could feel the extra ounces on my body and my clothes felt tighter. My jeans felt as though they shrunk a few sizes and my shirt felt snug around my arms.

In contrast, on days when the number went down, my mood skyrocketed and I suddenly became ecstatic. My eating disorder took control and made me feel like I accomplished a task, even though it was going against the road to recovery. I felt more powerful and I was more satisfied with my body.

We always knew when someone's weigh-in was good or bad. Our faces told everything, no words needed to be said. We never had to ask any questions because we all knew the feeling. The worst days were when we all were disappointed about our weights. Some were disappointed for weight gain and some for weight loss. But on those days, it took a lot of strength for us to participate in groups.

When I was disappointed, I tended to withdrawal and kept to myself. That was a common practice among all of the patients and so when we were all not having a good day, group therapy sessions were not as helpful as they could have been. It was hard to have a group session when none of the group wanted to talk. It was easy for us to get lost in our heads and completely ignore everything else that was going on around us.

The goal that my treatment providers set for me was to gain about a pound or two every week. That was not much at all for anyone who was not too concerned about weight, but for someone who made it her life to lose weight, it was a huge amount. I fought so hard and put my body through hell in order to lose those pounds and they were going to come back even faster than I lost them. My work was to be reversed and the monster inside scolded me for letting me put the weight back on. I did not like my doctors very much for making me gain the extra pounds. In comparison, it was extremely easy for me to have enough willpower to starve myself and it was extremely difficult to give it the nutrients it needed in order to get to a healthier weight.

My rationale was toyed with and I often convinced myself that the whole program was a set-up and that they were all only trying to make me obese, not healthy. Obviously, that was not the case, but irrational thoughts appeared out of nowhere. Many other patients believed the same thing. We often joked that our doctors probably were not at healthy weights themselves, and we doubted that they followed our meal plan. We were convinced that the people who were giving us advice were secretly a bit disordered themselves. Discussions were held at dinner and the conversations made our meals a bit more bearable.

Sara, an older woman in her 40's, started the debate one evening.

"I'm sure they don't even follow what they're telling us! They're skinny, there's no way they eat everything that we have to eat."

We laughed and agreed, not sure whether it was true or not. But Sara was not happy with her theory; she wanted to know for sure. During a group discussion about our meal plans and how food was important for our bodies, she chimed in and began to speak directly to Dr. Serrano.

"Do you even eat what you tell us to eat? Do you do what you tell us to do?"

She stunned us all with her bold bravery.

Dr. Serrano thought for a minute, taken aback by the very honest but very candid question.

"I wouldn't be teaching what I don't practice myself."

Her short answer sounded legitimate, although we still were not fully convinced. In our heads, any woman who was thin had to have some sort of eating problem. Because of the culture and the media, we were sure that about 98% of all females in the United States had some sort of disordered eating, and we were quick to judge and tried to point them all out. We made a game of picking out unhealthy coping skills in others, laughing and snickering as we bragged about what we had learned in therapy. We had become well versed on many different topics and knew much more about therapeutic techniques than most people.

We discussed many things in different therapy groups and on our own free time while waiting for groups to start, but we were not allowed to say any specific numbers.

Weights, calories, and all numbers were off limits in order not to trigger anyone else and their symptoms. I am glad the rule was in place, as I would probably feel jealous if another girl bragged about her caloric intake.

Eating disorders were notorious for being very competitive between two parties. One aspect of eating disorders was being the best, pushing the furthest, losing the most weight, eating the least amount of calories. The lack of numbers within our talks was very helpful in all of our progress.

Trying to gain weight was not as easy as I originally thought it would be. I thought that eating more normally would automatically add the pounds, only it was not that simple. Even when I did follow my meal plan and was pulling in quite a few more calories than I had previously eaten, my body did not respond in the way that I had imagined. I first gained some weight from the lack of water in my body. The first meals hydrated my body again and it showed on the scale. I was secretly happy about not gaining the weight, but in order to be discharged from the program, I needed to get to my goal weight first.

Eventually, a supplement was added to my meal plan. The supplement, Ensure, was a high calorie nutritional aid, and many people supposedly drank it on a regular basis. To me, Ensure was a creation of the Devil. The caloric and fat content was equivalent to a milkshake in my mind. I would have rather had a milkshake. The Ensure was a stamp that screamed, "I'm here for you to gain weight!" I did not see it as a healthy nutritional supplement but as fat and weight in a bottle. Ordinarily, it probably would have tasted good. But drinking it for the sole purpose for gaining weight tainted the taste and it was not enjoyable. I dreaded drinking my 350-calorie drink every night. It was a chore, and for once, I wanted to gain weight so I did not have to continue the torture of drinking the thick liquid.

The supplements did not take too long to add the extra pounds and I soon reached my goal weight. On one hand, I was excited and relieved that I did not need to gain any more weight. On the other hand, I gained weight! I was terrified that the number would keep increasing, no matter what I did. I imagined my body getting back at me for the constant beatings I had put it through, storing every single calorie and saving it for my future, adding extra pounds for no other reason than to mess with my head.

Being at my goal weight meant that I was no longer sick, I no longer needed help, I thought. Everything I had seen in the media was so focused on low weights and so I assumed no one would take me seriously if I did not look sick. I was worried enough when I was underweight and even more worried when I reached my healthy weight. I assumed that people would ask me what was wrong, and they heard my answer, they would respond, "But you don't look anorexic!"

Commenting on the appearance and weight of a person with an eating disorder was probably the worst thing anyone could do. No matter what that person says, the sick one will take it the wrong way. I never wanted to hear that I looked healthy; that meant I looked fat. I did not want to hear that I looked good; that, too, meant that I was fat. Everything and anything could be misconstrued and interpreted as being fat.

The program kept track of my weight and even though I knew my "official" weight on the hospital scale, I still struggled with the scale at home. I continued to use it quite frequently and it was not helping any. The outcome was slightly different from the hospital scale and that constantly played with my head. I wondered if I really gained or lost weight, and how much the scales were off. I used my scale at home more often than I should have. I did not need to step on the platform to find out what I weighed. I already knew how much I weighed, only seeing the number gave me a sense of control. If I felt anxious, it calmed me. I knew then exactly how I was doing in that exact moment and I did not have to worry about it any longer. At least, I did not have to worry about it for a while. The worry never really went away.

My treatment team urged me to get rid of the scale that had been sitting in the kitchen. It was the instrument that first started the obsession. My parents did not understand the impact that it had on my life. Seeing the scale every day, especially where it was sitting (next to my chair at the kitchen table), reminded me of my weight. Dr. Serrano compared it to a drug addict trying to stay sober.

"It's like sitting a syringe on the table in front of a heroin addict. They do not want to stick it in their arm, but they are very tempted to do so. As long as it is there staring them in the face, they will be tempted. It is the same with your scale. You will be tempted unless you get rid of it."

She explained clearly to my dad one night during a family group. Before the discussion, he had no idea how it made me feel. After her comparison, the light bulb lit up in his head.

"Oh. I get it now. I can see how that would be hard."

He finally understood something that I could not put into words myself. I was not good at explaining how I felt or why things affected me and hearing from someone other than me made him understand.

The night the discussion took place, he took action. I came home half-expecting the scale to be gone, although, I hoped that it would still be there for old time's sake. I walked into the kitchen and looked to the left. The scale was no longer sitting against the wall.

"Where's the scale?" I asked.

"I got rid of it."

"Oh...ok." I was not happy about the decision but I knew it was a step in the right direction for letting go of the control the scale. It had been holding too much power and its power had been taken away.

13

FAMILY DYSFUNCTION

One aspect of eating disorders and treatment that frustrated me was families. Family members just did not seem to get how eating disorders work or why they were used as a coping skill to deal with life. Sometimes, they said the most inappropriate comments to the one who was suffering. Yet, they did not know that what they said was hurtful. Communication between families and patients was a difficult battle in the lives of most of the patients, including mine.

My parents did not understand why I was putting

myself through such torture and they often wondered what they did wrong in order to cause it. My mom especially worried about what she might have done in the past to contribute to my self-starvation; and despite my insistence that it was not her fault, she continued to ask what she did.

"What did I do wrong?" she'd ask in frustration.

She did nothing, and most parents did no one specific thing. Certain personalities had a pre-disposition to developing eating disorders and I just happened to have some of those traits. Technically, I guess you could say it was my parents' fault, since I am made up of their genes, but that really stretches the truth.

In the program, we were allowed to bring our parents, family members, or friends to eat dinner with us once a week. After dinner, we all sat around in a circle and talked about various topics. Family members asked questions to help them understand better and it was our job to let them in on our little world. It was still hard for them to piece together how our minds worked and they probably will never know completely.

During dinner, we were required to eat everything on our tray, and our guests had to follow the same rule. My mom and dad had no problem eating the meal - my dad actually liked getting some free food - but there were others who were stubborn and hesitant to comply.

I was lucky enough to have a couple support people in my life that may not have understood, but tried to learn more about what was going on inside my head. They did not question the rules of the program and they happily obliged to finish their dinners. Others did not have the same support and it tended to trigger some patients, myself included sometimes. In order for a patient to grow healthier, those surrounding the one in need must not necessarily understand, but be supportive in any way.

There were quite a few instances when a parent would leave part of their meal on their tray, or start with less food than everyone else. We were challenged to eat what was labeled as a normal sized meal, so when support people did not do the same, it made us question why we had to do it. We were taught from an early age to follow what our parents did, and if they did not eat the full meal, why did we?

It was very frustrating to me when I would finish my meal and look over at the thin mother at the other side of the table. Her napkin was scrunched up on her plate, signaling that she was finished with her meal. Only, her meal was not complete. There were still bites of chicken and spoonfuls of mashed potatoes lying on her plate. I looked down at my clean plate and wondered why I needed to eat it all. It was not fair, although, through the process of treatment, I was soon learning that there were many things in recovery that were not fair. If I wanted fair, I would only end up in a worse place.

Not only did parents sometimes refuse to eat the same meal as us, inappropriate talk was also brought up during our family meetings after dinner. I assumed that parents would be intelligent enough and take the liberty of bringing up more triggering conversation in private. I guess I should not have counted on my assumptions because they proved me wrong several times.

"Why do we need to eat all of that food at dinner?

And why are their meal plans so big? That's a lot of food!" One mother asked after a particularly hard meal for quite a few patients.

Sitting in a giant circle, everyone looked at each other as eyes widened and whispers started traveling between the seats. I was baffled at the lack of education the parent had concerning treatment and proper conversation. I was also surprised at the ballsy question. The mother seemed oblivious to her horribly triggering question and looked around trying to find an answer. When dealing with patients with eating disorders, it was never okay to comment on the amount of food, especially directly after a meal. Especially directly after a meal in a room with very vulnerable patients.

Dr. Serrano took a breath and tried to tackle the question with the dietician's help. They, too, were thrown off by the mother's inquiry.

"Well...." she said, as she tucked her hair behind her ear, "...the meal plans here are designed following the food pyramid guide. The meal plans and each individual meal are no more than what a normal person should be eating every day. Because our patients only eat three meals and a snack, sometimes it seems like a lot because there are no snacks in between. Also, this country has been bombarded with so much information that it's hard for a lot of people to tell what a normal meal should be."

The mother was not buying her answer and for some reason felt the need to challenge the trained professional.

"Why do they need to have a dessert every day, though? No one eats dessert every day, or at least they shouldn't!"

The whispers grew louder and Sara was unable to keep herself silent.

"It's fine to have a dessert every day, they wouldn't lie to us. Everything in moderation is ok."

"Eating dessert makes us feel like it's more normal so we won't want to avoid it as much. Or it makes it seem like less of a forbidden food so we won't have the desire to binge."

I agreed with both of the women and wanted to add in my two cents.

"It's not like I want to have dessert. I do it because my doctors tell me to do it! We have to trust them since we can't trust ourselves yet."

"But..." The mother obviously did not understand the logic between meals, our requirements, our feelings, or anything else for that matter. She was caught up in her distorted views of eating and could not see clearly enough to know what was right to help her daughter. Her stubborn refusal to take in the comments by all of us made it difficult for her daughter to be around her. She could not get the support she needed in order to take steps forward in her process. Luckily, thoughts can be changed, and sometimes it took a while to reprogram.

It often made me upset that it was so hard for others to see what we all saw. In our world, things were turned upside down and inside out. Right was wrong and everything that we had been taught was turning into a lie. I had stepped into my own little distorted world of depression and self-hate many years before. That world was dark with little hope, with little chance of ever escaping. When I was trapped, I could not see outside of the misery. My brain had been rewired to believe that what I was doing was right, that it would fix everything and I would be happy. The lies that ran through my head eventually seared into my memory so that I could not forget. The fog was so dense that I could not even see the reality of the outside world. What others failed to see was that world of suffering. They could not know how difficult it was unless they had visited themselves.

Those who supported individuals who suffer from an eating disorder had a difficult task before them. Many times, communication between the support and the patient was so broken that it was nearly impossible for the two parties to get a message across. Communication with my parents was not the best and my mom often told me that talking to me was like walking on eggshells. I did not know how to express myself with words. She never knew how I would react to one of her questions, and so there were many times when she just avoided it altogether.

Then there were others who got too involved and crossed personal boundaries. Those that got too involved felt personally responsible for everything regarding the patients' treatment, only it really was not their problem. It was the patients' problem and no one else's. Others could help but it was a one man journey. It was hard for some to comprehend the complexity of such a disorder and so they tried to fix everything. It was not something that could be easily fixed and there was no easy solution and no easy way out.

The media and public opinions on eating disorders did not help situations, either. I realized that many families imagined that their daughter's story should have been like that famous-celebrity-who-had-an-eating-disorder-but-went-to-rehab-for-a-month-and-is-perfectly-okay-now.

Sure, sometimes there were those who were lucky enough to move past the demon within a month. But that was rare. It had been glamorized in society and it did not work that way. For some of the patients in the program, it was their way of life. Going in and out of treatment, year after year, was normal.

Doctor's suggestions were also challenged. Seeing things from a parents' point of view, I suppose that it would be hard to accept that the doctor's advice was more important at that time. In treatment, since family was not very well educated, some of their suggestions and comments had to be taken with a grain of salt. The professionals, on the other hand, knew what they were talking about.

Relationships with family could be a stressful situation and could even prompt symptoms. When I was walking through my dark world and looking for a way out, the last thing that I wanted to hear was my parents questioning anything I was doing. They did not necessarily need to understand, but they needed to be a little empathetic. Eventually, that empathy became an echo to follow and I started to follow the dim path out of the dark world. Without it, it would have been easy to stay lost and discouraged.

14

BOTTLE IT UP

A common trait among myself and the other patients in the program was that none of us ever learned how to express our emotions. If we did express our emotions, it was not in a healthy way. I was taught to hold everything in and pretend to be happy, no matter what. I was afraid to cry and I felt embarrassed if I let a tear slip out as I desperately tried to hold back the urge. Anger was just another emotion that I was unable to feel and express. I was afraid that if I got angry with someone, I would hurt their feelings and they would hate me. My insecurities held me back and I was merely a puppet with the strings being pulled by everyone else.

People pleasing was my natural instinct. It was easy to make others happy and give up my own wants in order to satisfy them. My sacrifices did not bother me at first, but they added up and I soon wondered whom I was really living for. I was not living for myself; I was living for everyone else. I realized that it was something that needed to be changed.

I did not believe that I was ever not worried about others judging me based on my feelings, reactions, and emotions. I assumed that to keep people in my life, I needed to be pleasant all the time and cater to their lives. No one saw the true me or how I really felt.

Bottled emotions were something that was talked about a lot during group therapy. No one was comfortable speaking her mind for fear of judgment and ridicule. Even though everyone in the world had emotions, we somehow believed that we did not need them. We were cardboard cutouts of real people, never responding truthfully to others. We walked around like real people, functioned like real people, lived in the world like real people. Only, real people showed what they were feeling on the inside, by expressing it on the outside. They were not afraid to open up their soul just a little bit in order to get closer to another person. We were emotionless.

A lot of the time when I wanted to say something during groups, I kept my mouth shut in order not to create any tension. I did not want to upset anyone else, even if my input would help in the long run. But keeping emotions inside was a threat to all of us. Bottling emotions was one of the factors causing the eating disorder in the first place.

As humans, we were programmed to feel and to emote. It was what made us human, it was how we were different from all other animals. Without emotions, we were not really human. Keeping the feelings inside only worked for so long until there was no room left for incoming thoughts. Eventually, the storage would run out and the emotion could no longer be hidden. Instead of dealing with the feelings of the moment, every other emotion that had been held inside came out along with it. In a split second, the volcano of feelings erupted and life became overwhelming.

The eating disorder was a way to escape that overwhelming feeling. In order not to express those emotions that were held inside for so long, the focus on food became a way to divert attention from the real problem.

Crying had always been the physiological response to an emotional situation. When a baby was hungry and needed food, he cried. When a child scraped his elbow on the sidewalk, he cried. When a boyfriend broke up with his long-time girlfriend, she cried. Crying made the emotional pain just a little bit easier. Somehow, the feelings became trapped in the tears and they disappeared as the salty tears dried.

I learned that crying was not so helpful, that it was not really that necessary. Instead of crying, I was used to keeping it all inside. My tears did not have a chance to go anywhere and I was drowning in years' worth of pent up anger, sadness, anxiety - everything that I forced myself to shut out. When the tears did slip out from my eyes, I tried to hide the fact that I was feeling anything. I wiped away the wetness and tried as hard as I could to put on a smile for others. Even alone, I felt uncomfortable crying. No one was watching but I still felt like I was doing something wrong.

It was rare to see someone cry during our group sessions, and when someone did, we all sat back and tried to think of a way to make her feel better. We were like deer caught in headlights, staring blankly at the situation in front of us, having no clue what to say or do. I did not feel comfortable consoling anyone who got too teary-eyed. Their emotions scared me and I was used to running away from situations like that. I was confused as to why it was so hard for me, until we shared our stories during one of our groups.

"Who here doesn't like to cry?" Dr. Reed simply asked as we all glanced around, wondering if we all felt the same way. One by one, we all raised our hands, and then giggled when we saw how similar we were. It was more of a nervous laughter since we were not talking about a particularly funny subject.

"Now, why don't you guys like to cry? It's normal. If we weren't supposed to cry, we wouldn't have tear ducts. Or Kleenex, right?"

We giggled again at her sense of humor and quietly thought about the question.

Sara was the first to speak.

"I don't want anyone to think that I need any help. I do not want my family to worry about me. I am able to take care of myself. I don't want to place my problems on anyone else's shoulders and burden them, they have enough to worry about."

Quite a few heads nodded around the room, including mine.

"Yeah. I feel the same way. I feel like I'm old enough to not bother other people with my trivial issues. There are so many other people in the world who have it so much worse and I shouldn't be complaining." Carrie explained, and again, heads nodded and we all agreed.

Dr. Reed was intrigued by the answers that were given.

"So, your problems don't matter because others have bigger issues to deal with? Who says that your issues aren't big and important to you? Why should you cheat yourself out of getting feedback from another person who could possibly help the situation?"

My answer came quickly and I spoke up.

"Well, they're important to me, I guess, but not important enough. Who wants to hear about my little problems? They're not anything huge and I should be able to deal with it myself."

"You're all "should"-ing yourself. When you do that, you're not seeing the situation itself, but what you should've, could've, would've done, making you feel worse."

Deep down, I knew she was right, but my mind wanted to argue against her reply. My stubborn side wanted to let her know that what I thought was correct, even though my truth was not very true at all. My mind loved to play games with me and to make me feel insecure and not so intelligent. I knew I was intelligent, yet somehow, the little voice was able to slip in and tear away at my confidence. It had been doing that for as long as I could remember. It was there before the eating issues, long before I ever thought of losing weight. That voice was what made me turn against myself.

Dr. Reed continued to try to let us in on her line of thinking.

"What happens when you shake up a bottle of soda, if you leave the cap on?"

It was an obvious answer and it did not take long for us to shout back, "It explodes!"

"Right. That's what's happening to all of you on the inside. Your emotions have been held inside for so long and eventually they will need to come out. All the built up emotion will come out at once and it'll be pretty intense. It's no wonder you've all learned to deal with things by distracting yourselves with unhealthy coping skills. Do they work? Sure. For a while, maybe. Do they fix anything? Nope."

I did not want to feel everything at once. It was hard enough to feel the emotions separately. There was no easy way to live with the emotions but I also knew that there was no way to live without them, either. I sometimes wished that I was a robot with a circuit board instead of a heart and brain. Robots did not have to deal with feelings. They also did not have to eat, which would have been just fine. But I was not a robot and I could not wish away my life. I was going to need to learn how to deal with things if I wanted to really live my life the way that I had always planned.

15

CELEBRATING WITH PAPER CANDLES

Today is my 20th birthday. I don't particularly like birthdays, but this one especially isn't a birthday I want to celebrate. I feel like 20 is such an in-between age. I'm not a teenager anymore, yet I'm still not an adult since I can't drink alcohol legally. Too bad 20 doesn't have a special meaning. It's not a milestone, I am just another year older. Turning another year older scares me. I feel like I'm behind every one else my age and I should be doing more things by now, but I'm not. I'm stuck in one place while every one else is moving ahead. I want to catch up and do whatever they're doing. I have learned through therapy that if I compare myself to others, I will always find something to critique myself on, but what I haven't learned is how to keep myself from comparing.

One advantage of spending my birthday while in the hospital was that I definitely had plans for my birthday, and friends in treatment would be there for me. One disadvantage of spending my birthday while in the hospital was that....well, it was in the hospital. At least it meant that I would be getting a free meal -- although, a free hospital meal was not much of a treat.

Meal times were, not surprisingly, sometimes very tense, especially for new patients getting used to the program. Dinner was also rough if we just came back from an intense therapy session, leaving us with upset stomachs and no excuse to get out of eating. Since we were in a higher level of care, but not there 24 hours a day, we had the privilege of making our own decisions for our meals. That was sometimes a difficult and demanding task.

I was convinced that the cafeteria deliberately messed around with us on a few occasions, giving us two entree options that had us questioning whether it was fit for human consumption. I was sure it was a sight to be seen as we all roamed around the tiny cafe searching for the best options. Our brains were calculating calories and estimating fat grams, and even though nothing was said out loud, an outside observer could tell we were all in our heads.

Half of the time, we had no clue as to what the Soup of the Day was, and the staff was no help to us in trying to figure it out. Some sneaky patients would try to get away with diet drinks or coffee but the dieticians always caught on to their tricks. We silently counted off each item on our trays since we all had a certain meal plan to follow. After we loaded up our trays with our meals, we all stood in line as the dieticians checked off what we chose. Standing in line was sometimes uncomfortable, as I assumed other "normal" people in the cafeteria knew why we were there. I pictured them whispering, "Look, there are those eating disorder girls!" I did not want anyone to know why we were there. But at the same time, there was a slight twinge of pride. We were a part of the Eating Disorders Club, and membership required ultimate willpower and dedication.

We all sat at a big round table in the dining room of the hospital cafeteria. Sometimes, it felt as though we were a big family, laughing at jokes and having conversations about college choices or what good movies were playing at the theater.

Other times, it was so awkward that I just wanted to crawl under the table to eat my food and stay there until the hour was over.

No matter how comfortable we were with each other, we were all still very uncomfortable with food in general. We were sometimes forced to eat items that we would have normally never eaten at home. The rules and authority intimidated me enough to gag down anything that I disliked. I had never liked mushrooms, but while in the cafeteria, I forced myself to eat them in order to not get in trouble. I did not want to be a bad patient. Others did not care too much about getting in trouble, and some intentionally broke the rules and rebelled against all authority.

Sophie, a normally shy girl about 17 years old, once threw a buttered roll across the table in the direction of one of the dieticians. Apparently, she was not thrilled about adding the extra fat (butter) to her bread. Our eyes widened and we waited for the consequence of her action.

We normally had two dieticians on duty, but that day, there was only one. Julie was newly hired and probably was not expecting a situation to occur within a week of her joining the staff. She was even tempered and spoke softly, traits that probably were a disadvantage to her when Sophie acted out. Julie calmly walked over to Sophie and led her to another room to have a chat. The rest of us at the table burst into laughter, knowing that throwing a buttered roll was very immature and childlike, but very funny at the same time.

Those types of situations did not happen very often but they were quite entertaining when they did. It provided some comic relief and eased the tension in the room, making it just a little bit easier for the rest of us to tolerate our meals.

We were not allowed to talk about certain subjects, in order to stay away from eating disorder and body image issues. Quite a few patients had been in the program before and knew of others who were in the inpatient program at the time we were in IOP. Even though we were not allowed to talk about other patients we knew, that rule often went out the window and current or former patients were mentioned by name. We wondered how they were doing, as we were all genuinely concerned about each other. We were all connected by our life threatening disorders and that bond was strong.

It humored us when the dieticians had to come over to our table and remind us not to talk about certain things. They sat at a table next to ours, usually working on paperwork, and listened intently as we quietly talked and ate our meals. Sometimes, we did not listen to them and it forced them to sit at our table for the remainder of dinner. We got a kick out of breaking the rules since there were a lot of restrictions. We were not allowed to drink coffee with our dinner, yet some of the coffee drinkers would try to sneak in a cup. They were always caught, but the fun of it was trying to get away with something.

Normally, on my birthdays, my parents and I would go out to dinner to celebrate. While in treatment, I had to have my birthday dinner at the program. I was not excited about that but I hoped that there would be cake for dessert, at least. To my surprise, the fridge was stocked with chocolate cake on my birthday. Since we were required to have a sweet dessert at each dinner, I grabbed the cake and informed everyone, "This is for my birthday!" A few others challenged themselves and took a piece of cake as well. We were all worried about the calories in the cake but since we were eating it as a group, we could support each other through the process.

By the time I finished my dinner, I was not too hungry for dessert, but I knew that I needed to find the strength to eat it. We were required to eat everything we chose or we would be written up for non-compliance. I stared at the mound of chocolate cake and for a minute got caught up in my eating disorder thoughts. I wondered how many calories were in it. I worried about the fat content. I was convinced that the slice was bigger than a normal slice and that the cafeteria food was fixed to make us gain weight.

Eventually, I calmed myself down enough that I had 15 minutes to eat it before we had to leave.

Since we were in a hospital, we were not allowed to have candles. Danielle came up with the genius idea of placing rolled up paper into the cake, representing candles. We used our imaginations to picture a few lit candles atop my chocolate frosting and they all wished me a happy birthday. Still stuck in our imaginary world, I playfully blew out the "candles" and thanked everyone.

Even though I was not at a restaurant of my choosing or celebrating my birthday with my real family, I was celebrating with my treatment family. They supported me and cheered me on as I finished the last bite of the chocolate sponge, and instead of feeling guilty about eating the dessert, I felt proud. I accomplished something that I would not have been able to do on my own just a few months before.

16

STEPPING BACK
INTO LIFE

It took a few months until I was stable enough to be discharged from the program. I did not expect my stay to be so long and I was excited to be leaving treatment. Since I was required to go to the hospital four times per week for four hours per day, I did not have much free time outside of the program. The therapy groups and worksheets that I worked on throughout the months had given me enough confidence in order to make improvements, at least enough improvements for me to be signed out. Even though I was excited to be leaving, I was also excited that I would not have a strict watch over my food intake or my weight. I could go back to controlling it, as long as it did not become too obsessive again.

I had acquired a thick binder filled with various handouts I received throughout the weeks. Many were aimed at building self-esteem, working through anger, boundaries with others, and how to deal with emotions by using healthy coping skills. If I was having a rough time and having any doubt, the papers would be there to guide me along the way. The binder was my emergency kit if I ever needed any support.

I also had created a wide array of artwork during my time in art therapy. One of my favorite projects was a mask I created out of plaster material, the kind of material that was used to form casts for broken bones. On the outside was my face, the face I showed the world, the face that smiled and did not look like anything was wrong. On the inside was how I really felt, bright red in color with intense words describing my true emotions. It was a powerful piece of artwork and it reminded me how of I presented myself to everyone else.

The projects collected in my art folder held an incredible amount of emotions, from depressed, to anxious, to excited, to everything in between. It was everything that I had held inside my body. It was an expression of me and my voice, of what I was holding back because of the fear. I could not leave the folder in the art room anymore. My artwork, along with every expression, had to be taken home with me.

On my last day, I was asked to speak in front of the

group to provide some insight for the other patients, and to give them encouragement. I looked around and noticed each person's face. Some patients had been there with me for my entire stay and others had just been admitted to the program and were only beginning their journey. Some others had left well before me or were kicked out because of insurance company policies. I saw in all of them a glimpse of hope and sadness. We were all there for the same reasons but no one ever said the process would be easy.

I coughed to clear my throat and swept my bangs away from my eyes.

"Well, I've been here for a while, and it's been really hard. I want to thank all of you for helping me and I know all of you have the strength to get better. I wish everyone good luck and I hope to never see anyone again. I mean, *here*, at least."

Everyone laughed and agreed we did not want to meet again in the same situation, in group therapy rooms being forced to talk about uncomfortable subjects. If I saw anyone again, I would want to see her while we were enjoying a coffee at the local Starbucks, not in a hospital.

Technically, we were not allowed to keep in contact with others who we met while in the program, although, we found ways to slide past that rule without any questions being asked. The internet made contact readily available. Knowing that I could have support through virtual means gave me a sense of comfort. I was not sure why it was discouraged for us to keep in contact since the interaction I gave and received outside of the hospital was supportive. I guessed that someone in the past must have abused the rule in some way, by using other people for support and then unintentionally dragging them back down into the eating disorder.

As my long stay came to an end, everyone, including the doctors and therapists, wished me good luck. Their encouraging words made me feel confident that I would not need to repeat the process I had just completed. I was proud of myself for managing to learn things about myself and new ways on how to cope in different areas of my life. I gained a ton of knowledge that would be very helpful in my future.

But I was also terrified.

Even though I completed the long journey, things were going to change for me. I would no longer have my days filled with hours of therapy. I was not going to see the same people day after day, nor was I going to get their support. I was going to need to keep trekking on my journey by myself without the constant watch of my actions. I was not sure how I would be able to keep pushing myself to go further on the path.

Change was always something that I have never liked to go through. Change made me anxious and I tried to avoid it at all costs. Transitions gave me reasons to worry and I often found myself feeling sick from my never-ending thoughts. Jumping to middle school from elementary school, and then to high school from middle school was an example of my rigidity concerning change. I was certain that everyone was just as anxious as I was, wanting to puke in the mornings from the stress build-up, trying to make up excuses to stay out of school. Not everyone was as anxious and I never learned how to deal with it in a healthy way. And until the tricks I learned in treatment, I had no clue as to where to begin managing it.

My routines worked for me, they were easy, they kept me from unwanted anxiety. Routine may have been boring but it was safe and I had always played things safe. Without the help of the program and those around me in the same situation, my world was no longer safe. I was stepping back into the real world where anything could happen. The real world was unpredictable. I knew what I would be doing every single day in treatment; however, in the real world, there were endless possibilities.

Possibilities also terrified me since I never failed to imagine the worst possible outcome happening to me. No matter the circumstance, I was sure that things would end up horrible and it would be my fault somehow. To avoid this, I usually did nothing at all, staring at the wall as the time passed by. I would need to make a change, yet I was not sure how to make the change on my own.

I was now alone with little support and my burdens were solely my responsibility. They always had been mine, although, I was able to pass them around, get advice, and lean on others for comfort. That was all gone and I was suddenly stranded in the same world that I had escaped in the first place.

I no longer had my eating disorder to shy away from the dramas of every day life. In order to stay on track, I had to use the tools that I was given in treatment. The tools were foreign and did not give me the same sense of relief as the eating disorder. They were helpful, but they did not make the feelings go away. Instead, I was forced to face them and sit with myself, unlike anything I had ever done before. I was used to hiding and pretending.

And even though I had plenty of tools at my disposal, I still yearned to crawl back to the eating disorder. I would have my freedom again and I could play the dirty game without being watched as intently. My new weight made me feel uncomfortable and I wanted to numb out like I had done before. The monster did not go away. It only became more quiet. Half of me wanted it to go away forever so I could live my life in peace without the constant whisper in my ear. The other half of me did not want to let the whisper to leave because it was like an old friend. Friends were supposed to stick together.

In order to stay on track, I was scheduled another appointment with Dr. Pitts. I had not seen him since before the program and I was not looking forward to seeing him again, but I did not have a choice. There was a long waiting list for therapy appointments and since I had seen Dr. Pitts once before, I did not need to wait. I thought that maybe seeing him would be better than not having any therapy.

I tried to stay positive about my upcoming session with him. Although my previous hour with him was not helpful, maybe things could change. I prepared myself for an awkward session but I hoped for the better to get something out of it.

On the exact time of my appointment, he strutted toward me in the waiting room, wearing almost exactly what he had been wearing the last time. The only difference was his tie, and his hair looked a bit shorter.

"Welcome back. Let's get started."

I forced a smile on my face and followed him back to his office. He now kept a few toys on the coffee table next to the patients' chair. My eyes were drawn to a colorful little chain. It swiveled around as I moved it through my fingers and it helped calm my nerves.

"What would you like to talk about today?"

I thought for a moment, giving myself a chance to dig my brain for a reasonable answer. I did not have a topic prepared to talk about.

"I'm not sure."

"Well, you were just discharged from IOP, correct? How do you feel about that?"

"A little nervous, but I'm ok, I think." It did not take very long at all for me to start giving automatic answers again.

Just like the last session with Dr. Pitts, it seemed as though the time stood still and I was getting nowhere by talking about surface issues. He did not seem genuinely interested in what I was saying to him. His lack of interest only discouraged me and my response was to stay quiet. I could tell that he was not the right therapist for me. We did not match up well but there was no solution to the problem. I had to deal with it and keep trudging through the mud with no trail to follow.

17

SLIPPERY SLOPE
ON REPEAT

My sessions with Dr. Pitts continued, despite my lack of interest and his unusual sense of humor. As the weeks passed by, my drive and motivation to recover was slowly dwindling. I discovered new reasons and excuses as to why I did not need to recover or why I did not need to have a meal. My excuses made sense in my head and to my eating disorder, but in reality, they were transparent and had no validity.

I used the excuse of being tired multiple times, day after day. Since my bed was so comfortable and I loved to sleep, I stayed in bed rather than fixing myself a meal and following the plan. As I bundled up beneath the covers, I felt a slight twinge of guilt. I knew what I was doing was wrong, but I wanted to rebel. I wanted to make my own decisions and I did not need any one telling me what I was supposed to do. Although there was guilt, there was also a sense of relief. Because I was not following the plan, I could continue to ignore my feelings. Eating brought up emotions; therefore, not eating suppressed them. It was an ideal situation, at least in theory.

Even though I felt some relief by rebelling, I also felt like a bad patient by not complying. People pleasing was my thing and not following the rules made me fear that I could possibly disappoint someone.

A few weeks after I was discharged from the program, I set an appointment with my dietician for the first time. She also had a waiting list because of the amount of patients coming into the center. I was not excited to start seeing yet another professional for help, but I put on a smile and dealt with it.

After yet another hour of talking in circles with Dr. Pitts in therapy, I met with my new dietician.

"Hey, Erin. I'm Melanie. It's nice to meet you!"

She was a down to earth type of girl who liked to smile a lot. Her job seemed like something she enjoyed thoroughly. When I saw those things in her, it made me feel even worse for slacking off with the program and my meal plan.

I wanted to make a good first impression. I did not want her to think that I was wasting her time or that I was being forced to meet with her. Although I still did want to hang on to my old habits, there was a part of me that wanted to continue moving forward.

She walked me back to her office, passing Dr. Pitts' office door on the way. Her walls were decorated with a few artistic black and white photographs, substituting for the lack of windows in the small room. I took a seat and she took hers at her desk across from me.

"So, I hear you were discharged from IOP a few weeks ago?" She flipped through my chart as she talked, then looked up at me and waited for an answer.

"Uh, yes. I think it was three weeks ago, maybe four, I'm not sure."

I noticed that my chart was opened to notes about my meal plan.

"How have you been doing with your meal plan, then?"

My eyes drifted over to the side and I had to think for a minute. My instinct was to lie to her, or at least, that was the eating disorder's instinct. Normally, I did not lie very often, but it was very easy for me to stretch the truth when it came to anything related to the disorder.

"I've been trying."

I was not lying, per se, but I was also not telling the truth.

Melanie caught on to my little trick.

"What do you mean by 'trying'?"

"I mean..." I could not keep eye contact with her. "Well, it's been hard. I don't have the support every day and no one is telling me the different things I should be doing. I

mean, my parents might, but I don't take them as seriously."
In truth, my food intake was not what it should have been.
Day by day, I had been dropping small things from my meals
so that in the moment, it was not a big deal. But those little
things added up quickly and I was soon not far from where I
originally started.

A look of questioned concern appeared on her face
for a moment. She pulled open one of her desk drawers and
found a worksheet that was very familiar to my eyes.

"Take a look at this. Tell me how much you've been
following."

The paper was a worksheet explaining the program's
meal plans: basic and standard. I was placed on the standard
plan, meaning that each of my meals had one extra item
compared to the basic plan. Other than that, they were
identical. Underlined on the sheet were a few reminders:

- Dessert every day! Everything is OK in moderation.
- Don't forget your caloric beverages! (Gatorade does
  not count.)
- Space out your meals appropriately.

Dessert was not that big of an issue for me. I did not
mind enjoying desserts and I thought it was funny that I was
required to have them when most other "normal" people
avoided them like the plague. What I hated were the caloric
beverages. The calories in drinks seemed to be a waste to
me. If I needed calories, I would have much rather eaten
them than drank them.

I realized that what I was eating was pretty far off

from what I should have been eating. I did not notice how many items I was missing until it was pointed out to me by Melanie.

"I'm actually missing a lot, I guess. I kind of wanted to lie and say that everything is fine and I am eating 100%, but I'm not." I was surprised at my honesty, especially since it was our first meeting. The part of me that really did want to recover decided to overtake the eating disorder side in that moment.

"Well, thank you for being honest. I know it can sometimes be very tempting to lie about these things." She was right. "Can I take your weight?"

I nodded, then stood up from my chair, slipping my shoes off at the same time. I walked over to the scale sitting in the corner of the room. I had not weighed myself since I was in IOP and my heart began beating faster in anticipation. My feet stepped on the scale and I waited for the beep to sound and the number to appear in bright red numbers.

As the machine calculated my exact weight, I closed my eyes in anticipation. My weight was supposed to stay stable if I did not want to face the possible threat of going back into the program. The number flashed on the screen and I let out a sigh.

"You've lost some weight. A pretty significant amount, I would say." Melanie jotted down the numbers on my chart and sat down in her chair again. My head dropped and I, too, took a seat.

"What do you think about that?"

Since I had been telling her the truth throughout our meeting, I decided to stick to the truth and give my honest answer.

"Honestly? I kind of like it, even though I know it's not a good thing. Like, I want to stay at my goal weight because that's the healthy choice, but my eating disorder tells me that I need to lose the weight. It's a battle every day and I never know if I'm making the right choice."

"Ok, well, thanks for letting me know how you really feel. I know it's not easy. But I am pretty concerned about the amount of weight you've lost since your discharge date. I'm going to have to talk to Dr. Hoffman about this. Admitting you back into IOP may be the next step."

I did not like that answer. I did not want to go back into the program. I already knew what was being taught and I would have nothing to gain. I could gain the extra pounds in an outpatient setting, I thought. I was really lying to myself, only I could not see that I was lying. Deep down, I knew that staying in an outpatient setting would not help me any more than staying at home. If I slipped that far in a matter of weeks, I could only imagine what would happen without a quick intervention.

After my appointment with Melanie, I chose to go to Starbucks and relax for a while. I always carried my journal around with me in my bag, and I liked writing while I sipped on a hot cup of coffee. I thought back to our conversation and the fact that she would be talking to Dr. Hoffman about my weight loss. A feeling of anxiety mixed with anger started to brew within me.

My anxiety arose from the simple fact that a decision was out of my control. Dr. Hoffman had the last word, he was the boss. Technically, I could refuse all treatment, but I knew that was not an option. I knew that if I refused it all, I would surely never dig myself out of the hole. I did not like the fact that he held the control, and I almost surely knew that he would agree with Melanie and recommend the program again. They were professionals and they had seen every trick in the book to avoid treatment. Any excuse that I could give would not be good enough. They were smart and they wanted what was best for their patients.

My anger came about from judging my performance between discharge and meeting with the dietician. I was angry that I could not stick to the program, but I was also angry that I did not lie to avoid any mention of going back. If I lied, I would have been able to dive deeper back into the sickness. A small part of me wanted that life back, even if I knew it was a horrible existence. My lack of ability to follow what I should have been doing frustrated me.

I felt as though my brain was two mismatched brains cut in half and sewn back together. The eating disorder was one half, the half that was evil and wanted me to self-destruct. It did not care if I headed down a path with no exit. The other half was my true self and knew what was wrong and right in reality. I was never sure which side I was supposed to follow. It was easy to think, "Eating disorder, just shut up!" in a moment when I was feeling confident and happy about myself. But when it spoke to me, there was nothing harder than trying to ignore it.

Slipping down the mountain I had just conquered was discouraging and came as a surprise. It was easy to make one minor slip, maybe two, but then they added up and it was no longer one tiny mistake. I had climbed to the top, looked around, and slid down to the bottom again. The slips were easy to ignore and it was easy to convince myself that it was not a big deal. By the time I caught on to what I was doing, it was too late and I had slipped too far down. I only had one logical choice: climb my way back up the mountain again.

18

NOTHING CHANGES
IF NOTHING
CHANGES

Before I had a chance to think too long about my situation, I was back in the Intensive Outpatient Program at Stafford Hospital. Dr. Hoffman, Melanie, and Dr. Pitts decided that it would be best for me to go back for another round. Of course, I was not happy about their decision, but I agreed to go any way. Again, a lot of my mind knew that the right thing was to stay on the healthy path, but I struggled to let go of the destructive behaviors. They were safe and familiar and change meant that I would need to survive the inevitable feelings of being uncomfortable.

I was embarrassed that I needed to go back to the program in the first place. I thought that a second try meant that I had failed, and failure was never an option for me. It never occurred to me that recovery was often a difficult process and was rarely a straight journey to freedom. In my head, since I did not get it right on the first try, I was a disappointment. The last thing that I wanted to do was to face Dr. Serrano and Dr. Reed. I was afraid that they would judge me for coming back, for not being able to handle the disorder outside of the programs' walls.

Going back into the program was almost as painful as stepping into the building for the very first time months ago. My anxiety was overwhelming even though I knew what to expect. But even though I was anxious, I was more willing to share my feelings with the group, something I had learned during my last stay.

While trying to calm myself down with deep breathing, a door swung open and Dr. Serrano walked out of her office, prepared to lead the first group of the day.

"Ready?" She glanced at us all and we started the march from the waiting room into one of the rooms for therapy.

We all took a seat around the large table that sat in the middle of the room. I sat next to the wall, as the wall gave me a sense of security. Dr. Serrano passed out a worksheet, and with little instruction, we quietly began writing.

My crossed legs started shaking up and down and

my fingers danced around on the flat tabletop. My anxiety was not decreasing with the passing time and the silence made the thoughts in my head even louder. I could not concentrate on the questions written on the paper. Instead, I used my pen to draw within the white spaces on the page. I drew leaves floating from the top edge down to the bottom, as thought they had fallen from a tree in autumn. After calming myself with a distraction, I was finally able to set aside my anxiety and focus on the worksheet.

The paper was familiar and I had completed it the first time I was in the program. Others in group were seeing it for the first time. The questions were based on our levels of motivation in our recovery process. On the top of the page listed the Stages of Change:

- Pre-contemplation
- Contemplation
- Preparation
- Action
- Maintenance

I had to think for a minute in order to properly place myself in the right stage. I was not sure if I was in the preparation or action stage.

The preparation stage meant that, "The person has made a commitment to change a behavior he or she considers problematic, and is intending to make the change soon."

The action stage was one step further meaning, "The person is currently in the process of modifying his or her behavior or environment to reduce or eliminate the problem identified."

Maybe I was not even as far as preparing, maybe I was still contemplating on whether I should go forward in the recovery process at all. I felt like bits of me were in various stages but I knew that I had a long way to go if I wanted to truly change. Not that I wanted to change my behaviors, but it was mandatory if I wanted to get out of the hell I had created for myself. I was in between wanting to step forward and keep going on my journey, eventually crossing the finish line, and staying where I was being miserable, yet feeling the comfort of that misery.

Any outsider would hear the word "misery" and automatically want to move forward and get away from it. It was not as easy as it may have seemed to others. The relationship between me and my eating disorder was almost like a relationship between a woman and an abusive boyfriend.

She loves him and he loves her back, yet he hurts her and knocks down her self-esteem. Deep down in the back of her mind, she knows that it is not right, yet she has trouble believing that he is wrong. She is scared to leave him and scared to stay with him at the same time. There is comfort in the familiar, even if it is hurtful.

By the time I explained my stage of change to myself, everyone else had finished writing down their answers and Dr. Serrano was ready to have a group discussion.

"I saw lots of writing in here today so I expect you all have a lot to say! Who wants to tell us what they thought about the Stages of Change?"

Like the start of many other discussions, the room was silent and every one was afraid to speak up first. During that time, I made sure not to make any eye contact, for fear of being called out to speak without warning.

But to my surprise, after a few moments of the silent questioning, I opened my mouth and began to explain what I had written on my paper. My analogy between my relationship between my eating disorder and a woman and an abusive boyfriend was told to every one. It was rare for me to give my answer first. I was usually too concerned about what others would think of my answer and so I always waited to respond after others so that I could gauge the situation and their opinions.

"That's very interesting, Erin. Have any of you thought about that before? About comparing those two situations?"

No one had thought about it before, and I started to feel like I was way off the mark. But then a few girls started talking.

"It makes sense. I just never thought about it."

"I agree. It's almost exactly the same, only the eating disorder isn't a physical person."

I quietly sighed in relief since my view was actually seen as something worth talking about. I was proud of myself for bringing up the subject in the first place, and even more proud for stepping out of my shell and doing what had been so uncharacteristic of me and starting the discussion. We all continued talking about my opinion and then switched to slightly different views throughout the hour.

About ten minutes before the group was finished, Dr. Serrano stopped us to give us a little pep talk. She liked to motivate us and we enjoyed listening to her honest advice. She did not sugarcoat anything but she was not harsh, either.

"So, today we talked about motivation and change. Motivation is such an important part of recovery and it's also one of the most difficult. You're all here, whether it be by force or your own will, and you all have a desire to change...but you all have a desire to stay the same, too. You're all expected to listen to us and our suggestions when your little devil is sitting on your shoulder telling you otherwise.

It's like we're telling you all to walk across this path of hot coals to get to the other side. We promise that it's better on the other side, but you have to get through the coals first. So you start walking, walking, walking, then stop. You're tired, and it's hard, and you want to go back, yet we tell you to keep moving forward. We know you still need to get through the tough stuff, but there's an end that seems so far away to you. We tell you that it's possible while the eating disorder tells you, 'Screw it, go back!' Your motivation keeps you moving and when it runs out, you're stuck, and there's no way you can get to the end."

She made complete sense to me. It also scared me because of how right she was. Putting recovery into images helped me see things more clearly, like my lens was focusing and the fog was lifting from my world. Instead of only hearing words, the pictures that she described burned into my brain and made things more real. It was easy to ignore words, less easy to ignore a graphic image.

She continued and wrapped up her pep talk.

"It's extremely easy to get caught up in the cycle of eating disorders. I've seen some of your faces multiple times. I'm not saying recovery is simple at all, but you are the only ones who can change. We can tell you everything and anything, health risks, statistics, predispositions, whatever, but we can't change for you. We can only help. You will stay in the same spot unless you do something yourself. I know Dr. Reed has told you multiple times, but I'm going to say it again. Nothing changes if nothing changes."

19

THAT CAN'T
BE ME

    My favorite part of the treatment process was art therapy. I had always been an artist, ever since I could remember, and my obsession with weight and numbers stole my passion for creating on paper what was inside my head. At nine years old, I asked Santa for a full art set, complete with paints, colored pencils, crayons, everything needed to draw and color. On Christmas Day, I found the set laying underneath the Christmas tree and I was so excited that I ignored all of the other toys that were there. As I grew older and technology advanced, I taught myself how to create art on the computer. I continued to pursue it during high school, and chose it as my major in college. Ever since the eating disorder took over, my decision to go in that direction had been questioned numerous times because of my lack of motivation and enthusiasm for it. But my love of art was coming back because of treatment.

While I was in the program before, I chose not to make a body tracing of myself. Body tracing was a project where patients drew themselves as they thought they were and then their actual bodies were traced over top of it. I was not in a place where I could process the work and I was not comfortable enough with the changes my body was going through. Although I was not thrilled about starting the project this time around, I knew it would be a good learning experience for me.

Without speaking about it too much beforehand, Michelle, the art therapist, already set everything up for me to work on my body tracing. After dinner one day, we all walked into the disheveled art room with the tables and chairs not in their usual spots. On the wall hung a sheet of paper that almost went from the floor to the ceiling. I looked at the paper, then at Michelle, and knew what was about to take place.

"So, Erin, are you ready to do your body tracing?" She knew that I was nervous about the project but she also knew that if she did not push me, I would not have to courage to ask to do it.

I grimaced and thought for a minute.

Was I ready to do this project? What happens if I draw myself and my drawing is actually smaller than my real body? What if I still hate how my body looks after seeing it in a different way?

I wanted to push myself, though, so I walked over to Michelle and grabbed the pencil she held out for me.

The paper on the wall was a huge clean white slate and I had to draw myself in the way that I perceived it to be. I dragged the pencil along the paper and my body slowly started to form, with arms and legs and eventually a head. I erased a few times, making myself bigger after each erasing. I thought that I was drawing myself too thin so I had to correct it. After about ten minutes, I stepped back to look at my body. It looked about right, I thought.

"Ok, Michelle, I'm finished."

She walked over with another pencil in her hand.

"I've been trained to do this so it will be accurate, alright? The pencil will stay level so it won't go in or out of your frame." She showed me how she would be holding the pencil, perfectly perpendicular to the wall. "Ok, I need you to stand right in front of your drawing...."

I stepped to the center and stood straight up.

"....alright. Just take a deep breath and try to relax."

My body was already tensing up as she started to trace, starting at the top of my head and working down my left side. I worried that the two drawings would be completely different, and that mine was the more accurate one. I was nervous that she could see my curves, something that I was not used to, as I always tried to hide underneath larger clothes.

About halfway though, she stopped and reminded me to take another deep breath. My fists had been clenched together the entire time and my legs shook from nerves. The second half of the tracing seemed to go by faster, possibly because I tried to focus on the painting across the room instead of the situation I was physically standing in.

"Ok, done! Now come back here and look at it." We both took a few steps forward so we were far enough away from the paper that we could see the full picture at once. At first, I thought she was playing a trick.

"That's not me." I scratched my head in disbelief and wondered how she drew the image with me standing in front of the paper.

"Yes, it is. You can ask anyone here, everyone saw me trace you. It's you."

My eyebrow raised and I walked over to the wall again. I turned around and placed my body against the paper, checking to see if the lines on the paper matched up with the imaginary lines of my body. They did. I was still in disbelief.

"I don't believe it. This can't be me. I mean, I know it is, but it doesn't look like me."

Everything that I had seen before had been a lie. Every mirror I looked into had given me a fake image. What I was seeing was not me, but a distorted me. My real body was a womanly shape with hips and a thin build. The body that I drew was a boxy character that looked to be overweight. When I saw the thin womanly figure on paper, I actually kind of liked it for a second. Until I realized that it really was me.

Why could I not like it regardless? If the body were of someone else, I would compliment her on her figure. Yet, because it was me, there were still parts that could be changed.

I no longer saw the image that was drawn on the paper, but the image in my head. I saw the disgusting body, my body that I had seen every day in the mirror. I reached over to the table and grabbed a bright red marker and I started marking the drawing with words.

Gross. Fat. Hate. Disgusting. Terrible. Horrible.

The words crossed my chest, arms, and legs, representing all that I hated about my body. It was what I felt when I stared back at my reflection in the glass. My hand scribbled some more over the shape and it was soon turning into a disastrous clash of misunderstanding. I wanted to cross out everything and not see any of it. I wanted to redo the entire piece and make it perfect and pretty. It was now ruined by my impulsive actions.

"What are you feeling?" Michelle asked quietly as she looked at my art.

"I'm kind of angry. I don't like this."

"What don't you like?"

I took a deep breath. Then sighed.

"It's like I've been lied to all of this time. Like, if that is what I really look like, why do I see myself so differently when I look at myself? I don't understand."

"You see yourself in a distorted way. It's not the real you, it's kind of like one of those fun house mirrors, you know? The ones where you're shaped all funny. We know those aren't real, but when you see yourself, it does seem real." She made sense and I knew she was right, but it still did not take away the anger I was feeling.

A smile appeared on Michelle's face.

"And you know what? You're getting your feelings out, your anger. I don't think I've seen you express your anger before."

I thought for a minute and initially tried to wipe the emotion off my face, only she already guessed how I was really feeling.

"That's true."

"And that's a huge step for you."

It was the first time during treatment that I was able to get angry at anything. Even if I was only getting angry at a piece of paper, I was still feeling the emotion. In that moment, I realized that something must have been changing inside me. Possibly, the monster was growing weaker and my own voice was growing louder.

20

JOURNALING
EXPOSES THE
SOUL

I've been avoiding journaling for almost a week now and am finally ready to type t all out....at least, I think I'm ready. While journaling in CBT last week about avoidance on these subjects, I physically felt sick and didn't want to think about t ever again. The sickness went away, but I've only thought about t more, making me very overwhelmed and anxious. I didn't eat well at all on Friday in order to cope with these feelings, even though I know that restricting will not help in the long run. What I need to do is face the emotions and feelings - but how can I? It may not be as painful typing out my thoughts, but how do I get past journaling? I can't get past the emotions by journaling alone. I will eventually need to talk and work things out. I've come to realize that maybe I am not supposed to deal with everything by myself. It obviously hasn't worked so far. I pretend I'm okay, tell myself that my problem is solved, stuff the feelings, then move on. But really, I deal with nothing and my eating disorder takes over in its place. I still automatically answer "Fine" when most people ask how I'm doing. Why can't I just come out and say, "Yeah, I'm really not okay." My treatment team needs to know exactly how I'm feeling or I will continue to be stuck.

Although I'm terrified, this is the first time in treatment where I've come this far and have seen something that can help me move on with recovery. During the past time in IOP, I tricked myself into thinking that I was feeling emotions and working through things. In the end, I knew I was going back to the eating disorder. For the first time, I am feeling real emotions and I know I need to get over this hurdle in order to start repairing myself. My eating disorder still tells me that I can go back to old habits after IOP, but I'm trying to fight it this time. This is the time when I need the most support ever. I'm barely treading water now and I'm afraid I will be discharged before I learn how to swim. Then the cycle will start all over again.

So what exactly is behind these emotions? I had t

all explained out in my head, but as I'm thinking this, I'm scared to actually write it and see it on the paper. I will literally have to face it. If I pretend I'm writing a story for now, maybe I will be okay....

I described in detail the situation between me and Randy, prior to being admitted into treatment. My treatment team was going to be let in on my secret that had been hidden away for so long. It was a relief to get it out of my head and onto the paper, but I was worried since I had not told anyone yet.

....maybe it was my fault? Maybe I should've yelled and screamed? Maybe I should've stopped him? Why wasn't I more assertive? We did drink and maybe I gave him some clue that I really did want to? He didn't rape me so why worry about it?

Looking back, maybe I only liked being around him because he was interested in me. It's hard for me to believe how anyone could be interested in me. I was just excited that someone took notice and I failed to set any boundaries. I let him take advantage. Things would've been different if I set my boundaries – and if I didn't drink alone with a guy at his place. By now, I've convinced myself that it happened, that maybe it happens to everyone and it's not such a big deal. I know that my body was shaking as I was driving home and that I was so scared in the moment, but maybe it really was nothing.

Instead of focusing on myself and trying to deal with past issues, I've been swallowed by the eating disorder and now I have no where I'm going. Or, I don't want to face what happened. What happens if the eating disorder goes away? I will have no wall to hide behind. I'd be exposed for every one to see, for every one to judge. Starving works since you feel so sick and dead that there's no time to think about feelings. Yeah, starving works, but t's not living. Sometimes, though, going through the motions and not remembering anything is much better than feeling. Actually, I would rather do most things than deal with my feelings.

Once I got to IOP for the first time, my fog started to lift and I was scared. That fog only lifted so high before I decided that t was best to keep t around. I've come to the point now where I know I need to face issues or I will keep repeating the cycle. Do I want that? No. But I don't want to face issues ether. Nothing changes if nothing changes.

Which is worse? I can't decide and so for now I'm stuck in this one spot, wanting to ask for directions but trying to find my own way.... and failing miserably. It's hard enough facing these things personally and I'm wondering how I will ever be able to handle anyone else knowing. How am I supposed to let people see this much of myself without completely breaking down? I want to break down and destroy myself and t's still in my head where t's been forever. I only want to run in the opposte direction and never come back. I feel sick and want to throw away this entry *and continue to avoid.*

With little eye contact, I handed my journal over to Dr. Serrano on my way to dinner one night. My stomach was upset during the meal as I thought about her reading my words on paper. I forced myself to down the food, trying to focus on nothing but chewing and swallowing.

As I walked back into the program after the meal, my heart pounded, wondering what I could expect, if anything. Luckily, art therapy was last so I had that to help take my mind off things. Did Michelle read it too? I wondered if she knew. I sat down and tried to gather my thoughts, but only long enough before Dr. Serrano opened the door and asked to see me in her office.

Oh, no! How could I face her? She read everything I wrote and she knew everything. Everything.

I took a deep breath, walked into her office, and sat down in front of her. I felt like she could see straight through to my soul and could see every secret I kept hidden inside of me. It was a very uncomfortable, vulnerable position to be in. But then she told me how important that one journal entry was to my recovery, how it was not my fault, how I have acknowledged an important event. I suddenly felt relieved yet still very vulnerable. I was no longer hiding behind the huge wall I had in front of me for so long. I was exposed.

"We're all very proud that you've taken this step in your recovery! Do you know how important this is? It's huge! None of us knew the extent of what you were willing to share with us, but this is a big step. How do you feel about it?"

"It's scary. I haven't told anyone, and I've never talked about it. I know that you won't judge me, but it's still kind of weird that you know. And it's weird that I know that you know. I mean, I'm sure it's a good thing, but I'm going to have to get used to it. I do feel relieved, though."

"I can imagine that this is a huge weight that's been lifted from your shoulders. It's not easy to face these types of issues, and it sometimes takes a long time, and here you are. You've taken a risk even though you were afraid."

Dr. Serrano assured me that my secrets would be safe and locked in her desk, but that did not take away the fact that my words had already been read and that they could not be taken back. I felt like my words were just floating around in space for everyone to see and I could not concentrate. My mind kept wandering and I kept thinking about what I had just done. I had taken a giant step and now there was no turning back. Now that it had been let out, there was no way to hide it away again.

I was more wary of making eye contact with the team because it was when I felt the most vulnerable. When I looked at them, I imagined a huge sign above their heads with, "I know!" written in big, bright letters. I often wondered if they saw me any differently, or if I had been judged negatively, or if....I did not know. Why did I even care? They were not my friends or family but they were all still important people in my life at that moment. I kept reminding myself that I was sure they had heard it all, and as professionals they needed to be open-minded on different issues. My instinct told me that it was safe that they knew and I was pretty sure they all realized it was a big step for me to be so open.

But then that little voice told me that maybe they were not so open-minded and that what I was being told was only to keep me content. For the most part, though, I was not too worried about them judging; rather, I was more anxious that my thoughts and secrets had been revealed to anyone. It had been comfortable keeping my secrets to myself and I did not have to deal with them. My eating disorder kept them far enough away that I felt safe holding onto them. I did not feel safe any more.

I had never revealed such important issues to anyone before and my treatment team as a whole knew more of my "real self" than any of my family or friends. It was such a foreign thing for me, to be so completely honest, that somehow I felt like what I did was something wrong. I was used to automatically telling people that everything was fine, and when I did have the courage to tell the truth and that I was really not okay, I felt the need to apologize. I did not want people to know the real me or that I was not okay most of the time. If people knew who I really was or how I really felt, I feared no one would ever want to be around me. It had become second nature to always pretend to be fine, to wear a smile all the time, and there was no way I could pretend anymore. The team knew exactly what was going on and it would have been pretty much impossible to be completely fine until the problems were resolved. I had to continue to be truthful.

I felt as though the situation as a whole was my "A-ha!" moment for my recovery. Dr. Reed told me that the team was excited that I had finally come out with important things to work on, but I wished I could have been as excited about it. It was the furthest I had come so far, and maybe the only real work I had completed. Maybe the past time in the program was a waste of time; or, maybe I was very slowly peeling back the layers to get to that point. I had no idea why I had finally come to that point. I heard the statement, "Nothing changes if nothing changes." and for some reason, that somehow made the difference. I was only starting to become comfortable with the treatment team knowing my deep secrets, so what was the next step? I was not too sure.

Even though I was not sure what the next step was, I had come to the realization that everything had nothing to do with my weight at all. I knew that for a long time but I did not really "get it" until I let everything out. Obviously, it was much easier to focus on weight rather than dealing with issues. Weight could be changed but feelings could not be changed.

During the days after I gave my journal to Dr. Serrano, I did restrict and I did wonder if I had lost weight. But then I thought to myself, *Who cares if I lost weight? I have important things to figure out here and the number on the scale doesn't mean shit.* Weight was such a trivial issue to worry about, but I guessed it seemed like the most important thing in the world when it was used to cover up the real issues. Many things seemed trivial to me when compared to the fight I was battling.

For so long, I had ignored the incident with Randy. Since my thoughts were written down and other people knew, it all became very real. Too real for me to handle at that point. I had no idea where to go from there and I was stuck treading water. I did not want to move any further. How was I supposed to come to terms with the reality? I could not accept what happened and I could not accept myself. I had rationalized my thinking and told myself that those things were not a big deal. I tried to pretend to be someone else and be happy. I thought of never telling anyone, just because of the fear of rejection and judgment. I came out with it but I did not think that I was strong enough to do much else.

How was I supposed to accept myself? It was so clear why it was hard for me to accept myself and the reasons were staring straight at me. I needed to find a way to turn around my thinking, even though I had not been successful with that yet. I hated myself for letting him take advantage of me. I hated myself for not setting boundaries. I hated myself for being ashamed and hiding. I hated myself for many things. I was never good enough and I always wanted to be like someone else, just so I was not me.

Those things would have seemed so illogical if I heard it coming from a friend. I would have told them that it was not their fault, that it was not a choice, that it was their life and it was not their job to keep everyone happy. But because it was me, everything was my fault and I would have rather suffered than disappoint others. I had hated myself for as long as I could remember and it was hard to believe there would be a day when I would be okay being me.

I was sure my head was going to explode, either from all of the emotions or from the headaches I kept getting from thinking so much. I felt so alone and I had no one to talk to about what I was going through. I talked in vague terms to Dr. Pitts during an appointment and I could only say so much without giving details.

I was very worried that I would be discharged out of the program before I was ready. I knew I was only treatment in order to stop eating disorder behaviors. I had previously been hesitant about discharge, but that time was a whole different situation. Before, I was anxious about not having the program for structure. I was still anxious about that, but I was also very worried that I would not have the time to be able to work through issues while still in IOP. Was I supposed to do the real work in outpatient? That support would not have been enough. I had not gotten to the point of actually talking about things and I hoped that would happen before I left. I had yet to say anything out loud to myself. Talking was admitting. Talking required interaction with someone else in the moment and it was so much easier for me to write. I did not need to see the reaction to my writing, but I did have to face the reaction when speaking.

I knew it would not be fixed before discharge and it would take a long time to work through after discharge, but I needed the support system. I was emotionally worn out. I could not say that I did not want to go back to the eating disorder once I was out because I was sure the urge would always be there when things got rough. But I just could not repeat the cycle again because then all of the work would have been tossed out the window.

I could have either chosen to ignore, turn around, and destroy myself. Or I could have faced it, move forward, and be healthy. I did not particularly want to do either. I had already been down the path of destruction several times and I never made it to the other side, so maybe I needed to go the other way for a change. Only I was terrified to go alone.

21

FEELING THE
FEELINGS

Now that I had faced issues, it was impossible for me to turn back around. I was walking on the hot coals on the path of my recovery. I saw my treatment team standing on the other side of the path, waving and encouraging me to keep walking. They assured me that I would be okay, safe, and that things were better on the other side. I could not fully trust them, yet I continued to walk, despite my trepidation. Slowly, but surely, my feet took me over the hot coals and I started to inch my way to the end.

My eating disorder was on the starting end, yelling

at me to come back. It wanted to keep me trapped and on the path of destruction. It was almost impossible to turn my head toward the better direction and ignore it. Every once in a while, the voice was very tempting and I made a few slips. But a slip did not mean a relapse. The monster had a way of convincing me that things would be different the next time. Maybe his way did not work previously, but I just had to try it again and I would see different results. I was promised that the next time would be the time that I would be happy. The next time, everything would be fixed and I would be content. It was not easy to ignore those enticing calls.

By disputing the eating disorders' challenges for me, the result was me being able to feel emotions. I had not felt true emotions for such a long time and it was very overwhelming. I did not like the change and I was not sure if I was supposed to be feeling that way. I questioned whether everyone was supposed to feel emotions that intensely. Luckily, I had the support of my treatment team in the program to help me through the intense times.

It was common for us as patients to be worried about feeling emotions. It was a foreign experience. Emotions were natural to others, but to us, it was a scary thing. Eating disorders muted out all feelings so that individuals did not feel anything at all. Happiness was shown as a smile on the face, but no real excitement was felt on the inside. Anger was ignored, not felt, and piled up inside, ready to explode whenever the emotions would come back. Depression was the only emotion that was present. There was nothing to live for and nothing to be excited about. It was a lonely existence with no emotions, yet, they were not wanted, either. It was a catch-22 that made all of our actions that much more complicated.

Dr. Serrano often explained emotions when one of us would start feeling again. We were confused as to why they were so intense, more intense than we had ever felt before.

"Emotions are like a wave." She drew a water line on the whiteboard with a blue marker. In the middle, she then drew a vertical line.

"I'm not an artist, but...what do you think this is?"

We examined the simple artwork on the board and came to a conclusion.

"It's a dam?"

"Right! It's a dam, blocking the water. Emotions are the water. They are built up and keep getting higher and higher until the level is equal to that of the dam. What happens then?"

"It overflows? Breaks?"

"You guys are smart! It either flows over the wall, or breaks from the pressure of the amount of water. Some of you are working through issues; the issues are your dam. For so long, you've built up this wall in order to block the emotions. If you're working on the issues, the dam is being chipped away, leaving the water no where else to go. It rushes through or over and all of a sudden, the emotions seem to come at once."

Her explanation made so much sense to me and I wondered why I had not thought of it before. My water level was so high that is was barely being held back by the dam. By acknowledging my secrets inside, the dam was being broken down. My flow of emotions burst out through the wall and overwhelmed me. I was literally drowning in my feelings.

I was not sure how to navigate through the waters. I was simply floating around, trying to tread and keep my head above the surface. I was never taught how to swim and so I was going to need to learn how on my own. I had the help of the professionals, but I felt alone. It was my journey and only I could free myself.

There was not an option for me to reach out for the life vest. My life vest was the eating disorder. I knew that if I reached out, I would not be able to let go again. The eating disorder had sneaky ways of trying to get back to me, but I was catching on quickly to the tricks.

Dr. Serrano continued her explanation of emotions and water.

"It's just like a wave." She drew a blue wave on the whiteboard, and wrote atop the crest, "Emotion."

"When you're experiencing, it's just like this." Her finger pointed to her drawing as we paid attention to her clever analogy.

"The crest of a wave never stays there for very long. It comes to a climax and then crashes down and disappears. Your emotions are exactly the same. It builds up until it crests, which is when you're feeling overwhelmed. In reality, emotions only last for about two seconds. That's it! The overwhelming sense makes it feel so much longer and ruminating tends to happen. If you let it happen naturally, it goes away. Without ruminating on the emotion, it dissipates, and another wave comes along. You're able to stay at the crest if you try, only that's not how we're biologically programmed."

If I wanted to keep heading in the right direction, I had to come to terms with the fact that I was supposed to feel. I was programmed to feel emotions, not suppress them. Suppressing them only made things worse, not better like I had hoped. My hopes had crumbled before my eyes. For every wish came a failure. The promises that were told to me were only lies. It took me too long to want to walk away from the monster. Suppressing the emotions only built them up and made them even more intense when it was time to feel. I could no longer ignore what was a natural human function.

I could not turn back around. I started to see the light on the other side of the path and it gave me hope, hope that I knew would be for real. The eating disorder gave me false hope and constantly played tricks on me. I was increasingly becoming fed up with the mind games, but I also was not sure if I could trust myself, with myself. I was not sure what was right or if I was going in the right direction. If I did not listen to the monster, who could I listen to? I was not confident enough in myself, so I chose to trust my treatment team until I could gain confidence. I decided to go the "Fake It 'til You Make It" route and pretended I knew where I was headed, when I was actually blind with no sense of direction. My only option was to listen to those who believed in me when I could not believe in myself.

By the time I figured out my plan of action, I was soon to be discharged from the program again. I was reliving a scenario I had just lived a few months before, only it was somehow different. The nervousness about being out of the program was not nearly as strong as it was the first time. I was not thinking about how fast I could lose the weight again or wondering when I would be back. My preparation and my willingness to try something different was scaring away my eating disorder. It did not like when I had control; when I was in control, the eating disorder voice was next to silent. It was there, yet not overwhelming like it always had been. I was playing the tricks, and I wanted to win the game. It was my turn to hand out the cards.

Before I could leave, I had to prepare a plan for my treatment. The plan was to be set in place to increase my chances of success and to minimize the risk for relapse. I did not want to have to be readmitted back into the program within a matter of weeks. Ideally, I wanted to stay out of the program for good. My plan was to stay well enough that I would not need intense support every day. I was not kidding myself - I knew that I would still need support - but I also came to the realization that maybe I was strong enough to overcome my obstacles. If I was strong enough to hurt myself, I was strong enough to make myself better.

I knew that something had to be changed within my support system in the outpatient setting. My dietician, Melanie, seemed to know her stuff. Although we met only a few times, I was confident that she would be able to help me during our appointments. I was also confident in seeing Dr. Hoffman, as I had seen him since the beginning of my journey. He scared me in the sense that he held the power, but that also made me want to work and stay on the positive side. Dr. Pitts, however, was a different story.

I had always assumed that the relationship between a

therapist and the patient did not matter too much, that it was just a professional setting and the two did not have to be compatible. I was wrong. My journey had taught me that in order to make progress, the relationship did matter. My therapist was supposed to be someone who I liked. They were going to be listening to me week after week, and I knew that I needed to be comfortable with them. I was not comfortable talking with Dr. Pitts and from the first session on, it did not seem like a good match. Sometimes I would get annoyed with his comments and dry humor. Although I liked to laugh, some jokes in therapy were not funny, sometimes even inappropriate. I did not feel like he was really listening to me. I felt that he simply heard my voice but did not pay attention to my explanations. I needed someone who I felt comfortable with, someone who would listen to me, someone who I actually wouldn't dread going to see every week.

As I signed my name on my discharge papers, I was not anxious. A sense of calmness washed over me, almost as if my body sensed that it was the end of that particular process. I was not finished the journey and I still had a long way to go, but I overcame obstacles that stood in my way. I never thought that I could conquer them. Before I could leave the program, I met with Dr. Serrano for one last meeting.

"So, Erin...it's your last day. How are you feeling?"

I clasped my hands together and a small smile appeared on my face.

"I'm kind of excited. I'll miss the people here, but I feel ready for the most part. It's different than last time. I'm not really expecting to come back. I hope I don't have to come back."

"Well, that's definitely a change from last time." We exchanged smiles and she continued.

"Since it is your last day, I don't really have anything for you today." Usually, in individual meetings, daily and weekly goals were set. We all met every day with a staff member so we could let them check in on us.

"You have everything set up for your outpatient appointments, right?"

"Kind of...." I fidgeted a bit and my foot began shuffling on the ground.

"I kind of don't want to see Dr. Pitts anymore. I'm not comfortable with him. I was wondering...if it's possible, can I see you instead?" I was slightly worried that she would not be able to be my therapist outside of the program, or that she did not want to be my therapist. My insecurities were still there but I pushed them aside just long enough for me to ask the question. I was comfortable talking to her and I knew that meeting with her instead would keep me on the right path.

She thought for a moment.

"The only problem with that is, you'd have to talk to Dr. Pitts about it. I know you've had some problems with him. You're going to have to be assertive and talk to him in order to make the switch. And I know being assertive is difficult for you. Other than that, I don't see why not."

Her answer pleased me, yet I started to worry about talking to Dr. Pitts about my decision, a decision I had not even mentioned to him.

"Yeah, that will definitely be hard. I don't want to hurt his feelings, but I know it's the right choice. I'm not looking forward to talking to him about it." Assertiveness was a topic that we went over numerous times in the program and it was still very hard for me to take in the concept. It seemed easy on paper, but in the situation, it was not easy at all.

22

TRUE TEST OF WILLPOWER

My last day of the intensive outpatient program at Stafford Hospital was on a Tuesday. That Thursday, I met with Dr. Pitts. I knew that it would probably be our last session together, although, I do not think he had any idea what was coming. My nerves made my stomach nauseous and my hands shaky. No matter how many calming techniques I had learned during my time in treatment, I was still unable to control my anxiety for the most part. I was always an anxious individual and it was going to take a long time to rid myself of its effects.

While sitting in the waiting room, my hands could not stay still. I played with my key ring in order to keep them occupied. My mind was still racing with thoughts and I had to convince myself not to back down. I knew I was making the right decision, but I was also scared of hurting someone else's feelings. My tendency to please others was still a part of me and it was a hard habit to break. The thoughts in my head kept going back and forth, ultimately giving me a headache from the intense thinking. As I saw Dr. Pitts walk down the hall, my heart raced faster and I knew that my moment was soon approaching, making the knots in my stomach even worse.

Our session went on for about a half an hour until a long pause. I had nothing to talk about and was still weary of bringing up the subject of terminating therapy with him. Up until that point, our conversation consisted of very trivial issues. I also had a terrible time of paying attention to what he was saying, and my words spewed out of my mouth without much thought. After a few minutes of silence and playing with the string on my jacket, I finally built up the courage to speak.

"I'm not sure how to say this...." I could not believe that I was actually going to tell him. My anxiety increased almost to the point of forgetting what I was supposed to talk about. His stare only made me want to shut up and continue on with the mindless conversation, but somehow I found the words to continue.

"Well...I was thinking..." He continued to stare, wondering what I was about to say. I did not usually bring up subjects in therapy.

"I was thinking....maybe it would be better if I saw Dr. Serrano instead. I mean, I'm more comfortable with her and I think it would help me a lot. I don't want to hurt your feelings...but....I want to see her instead."

I stared at the floor in order not to look him in the eye. I was convinced that he would be upset or angry. His reaction was better than I had expected, but still not excellent.

"Why do you think that? Therapy isn't about being comfortable."

I asked myself, *What is he trying to get at?* I had no answer for his question. I was not sure if it was rhetorical or genuine.

"I'm just more comfortable talking to her. And I think that's what I need."

"Hmm...well. I am not sure."

He was not sure? Was he not sure if I could see her? I was not asking him if I could switch, I was telling him. I was the patient and I had the right to switch.

"I just think it would be better." The only explanation I had for him was that seeing her would be a positive change for my recovery. Imagining future sessions with him only gave me the picture that I would continue to repeat the cycle of sickness.

He was silent and I had nothing else to say to him. In being assertive, one of my fears had come true: confrontation. I disliked confrontation more than anything and I avoided it at all costs. And there I was, sitting in a small room with someone who was not agreeing with me. But I was still alive. I had the strength and courage to speak my mind and to let him know what I wanted, and even though his reaction was not ideal, it was not the end of the world. I was able to let others know how I really felt and life was still going to happen, no matter their reaction.

The silence in the room grew more and more uncomfortable with each passing second. I continued to play with the string on my jacket, twisting the fabric and knotting it every which way. Playing gave me something to focus on. Without it, I was not sure what to do. We continued to sit in silence until the end of the hour.

"Our time is up." He broke the awkwardness by telling me that I could leave. I had to keep myself from running out of the room and escaping, never to turn back again.

We both stood and I walked toward the door.

"Thanks for your help." I was not sure if that was an appropriate comment to say to a recently fired therapist, but I went with it.

"You're welcome." he said, as he held the door open for me.

I rushed down the hallway and into the bathroom next to the waiting room. I used the sink to splash some cool water on my face to calm myself down. My nerves were finally decreasing and I could feel the relief increasing. My reflection in the mirror looked back at me and I saw a hint of a smile. I had just overcome another obstacle. It was another barrier standing in my way and I tore it down.

During the days following that final session, I was able to stick to my meal plan and use coping skills in order to keep the monster in check. It was not getting any easier and I was not sure if it would ever be easy, but I taught myself how to take things one day at a time. One meal at a time. One bite at a time. It was strange being away from the program in somewhat of a different mindset. It scared me and excited me at the same time.

On the days where I would have been at the program, talking in group, eating dinner with the others, I wondered how they were all doing. I was happy to be on the outside, yet I missed the interaction with the other patients. We understood each other and we knew what we were going through. I did not have anyone outside of treatment that could relate to me in the same way. And although I missed the friends I had made, I also knew that I would still have support from my outpatient team.

Before I knew it, I was back at Stafford Hospital in the waiting room, yet again. I looked at the dark walls and the modern decor, and I flashed back to the first time I sat in that room. In my mind, I replayed everything that I had been through in the many months since the start. I was a year older and wiser. I was still afraid of many things, but I was not as scared of myself anymore. I had grown to learn many things, and I learned that I had underestimated myself. I was much more capable of accomplishing things in life than I realized. When I looked at the other girls sitting in the waiting room beside me, I no longer envied their bodies. My comparing was not erased but it had decreased significantly. Nothing was going to change overnight.

Deep in thought, my ears focused on the sound of keys jingling. I heard footsteps walking down the hall and when I looked up to see who it was, Dr. Serrano came around the corner to bring me back to her office.

In her office were a few toys and motivational items scattered around. The window overlooked the parking lot, which was not a great view, but the sun was able to shine through. I sat in the chair with the pillow across from hers and let out a sigh.

"So, what would you like to talk about today? It's your session, it's up to you."

It was my recovery. My choices and my actions would determine my path. It was all up to me. I was not cured but I was on my way. I was not sure whether I would slip up again or not. I was not sure if I would ever need to go back into the program. I was not sure of anything, really.

For so long, I had been listening to the whispering voice and ignoring my own. I was finally starting to raise that voice enough to be heard.

AFTERWORD

I wrote this book for National Novel Writing Month 2009. Every year in November, thousands around the world write for thirty days, ending at the stroke of midnight on the 30th, with 50,000 words. I was one of those thousands of people setting aside other plans in order to write. Writing a book has always been a dream of mine, and now I guess I can cross it off my bucket list. I am amazed that I was able to accomplish such a feat and I am proud of myself for it.

This book is based on my own experiences with battling an eating disorder, going through treatment, and the thoughts behind the process. Technically, what I have written is fiction. Names have been changed but the general ideas and events are mostly true.

I decided to write about this in order to give another perspective on eating disorders. There are many, many books out there that focus on the subject, but not all of them go beyond the physical aspects. There are some that use shock value in order to pull in readers. And while that is good for publicity, it also does not speak the full truth. I intentionally left out specific numbers and weights because while eating disorders call attention to them, they are not all about the numbers. The common misconception is that eating disorders are used just to get skinny. While that is not completely false, there are many more reasons people turn to eating disorders to cope with life.

My battle is not over and I have been fighting for quite a while. My journey began in 2004 and I spent much of

2008 and 2009 in and out of the hospital, leaving me and my family to deal with insane medical bills. I have missed opportunities and years of my life because of the sickness, but I hopefully have many years to make up for it. There have been many times when I thought that I could never dig myself out of the hole I had created. I am still climbing out of that hole but I am not longer alone at the bottom with no light. I can see some of what is ahead. I am still crossing those hot coals and there are people waiting on the other side for me. Sometimes it is fun to look back and wave goodbye to my eating disorder. Sometimes I turn around and step in the wrong direction again. But in all of my struggles, I have learned many things. I believe that we are given obstacles in life on purpose. I have been able to learn about myself while others my age may not truly gain insight until much later. I have missed out on a lot, but I have also gained a lot in the process.

As in the book, my treatment team has played a huge part in my recovery. Although it is ultimately up to me, they have learned the difficulties and complications an eating disorder brings to an individual. I am less alone with them. I am thankful to have such a great team, although, I do not think the eating disorder is quite as thankful. The eating disorder is still learning how to listen to me.

RESOURCES

SOMETHING FISHY
http://www.something-fishy.org

NATIONAL EATING DISORDERS ASSOCIATION
http://www.nationaleatingdisorders.org

THE JOY PROJECT
http://www.joyproject.org

F.R.E.E.D. FOUNDATION
http://www.freedfoundation.org

THE CENTER FOR EATING DISORDERS
AT SHEPPARD PRATT
http://www.eatingdisorder.org

GÜRZE BOOKS
http://www.bulimia.com

JENNI SCHAEFER
http://www.jennischaefer.com

CAMPAIGN FOR REAL BEAUTY
http://www.campaignforrealbeauty.com

NATIONAL NOVEL WRITING MONTH
http://www.nanowrimo.org

ABOUT THE AUTHOR

Jennifer Kinsel is a twenty-something year old artist/designer/creative/dreamer. *Restricted: a novel of half-truths* is Jen's first book, a challenge she took upon herself for National Novel Writing Month; writing a book had always been on her long list of things to do before she dies. Born and raised in Baltimore, Maryland, she attended Stevenson University and earned a bachelor's degree in Visual Communication Design.

Since college, her life has taken a different direction than most her age, due to her battle with an eating disorder. Although the process of recovery is very difficult, Jen is hopeful that the obstacle was put there for a reason.

On a less serious note, she stays awake much too late for her own good, enjoys thrill rides and the rush of adrenaline, and watches The Golden Girls every morning while eating breakfast.

For more about Jen, visit http://www.jenniferkinsel.com.

Made in the USA
Las Vegas, NV
16 June 2021